SCOTNOTES
Number 20

The Scottish Ballads

Sarah M. Dunnigan

Association for Scottish Literary Studies 2005

Acknowledgements
I would like to thank generously the following people who have all helped me in writing this Scotnote: Ronnie Renton especially, for his patience, support and invaluable advice throughout; Lorna Smith, for her most useful and meticulous suggestions; the Schools and FE Committee of the ASLS; Duncan Jones; the staff of the Library and Archives of the School of Scottish Studies, Edinburgh University; Randall Stevenson, Head of Research in English Literature, Edinburgh University; Dr Kirsteen McCue, for her all her advice and suggestions; Sheila Douglas, who willingly shared her vast experience and knowledge of ballad traditions with me, and offered warm hospitality; Dr Rhona Brown, who kindly compiled the Suggestions for Further Reading and Ballad Recordings; especial love and thanks are for Anna and Matthew Dunnigan, and for David Salter, who have contributed in innumerable ways.

Published by
Association for Scottish Literary Studies
c/o Department of Scottish History
University of Glasgow
9 University Gardens
Glasgow G12 8QH
www.asls.org.uk

First published 2005

© Sarah M. Dunnigan

A CIP catalogue for this title is available from the British Library

ISBN: 0 948877 66 9
ISBN-13: 978 0 948877 66 7

Subsidised by

Typeset by Roger Booth Associates, Hassocks, West Sussex

CONTENTS

	Page
Prelude	1
The Debateable Lands of the Ballads	1
Across the Threshold	1
Introduction	4
What is a Ballad?	4
Encountering Ballads: Different Experiences	5
Ballads and Music	5
Do Ballads have 'Authors'?	6
Defining the Indefinable: the Ballad 'Text'	7
Ballad Form, Structure and Style	9
The Ballad Stanza	9
Ballad Patterns	10
Ballad Narration and Storytelling	15
The Drama of the Past: Telling History through Ballads	23
Ballads at the Frontiers of War	24
New Stories from Old Facts	26
The Passions of History: 'Edom of Gordon'	27
'Quiet' Voices of History: 'Marie Hamilton'	28
The Worlds of the Supernatural	29
Witches	29
Ghosts	30
The Devil and Malicious Enchantments	32
Ballad 'Morality' and the Psychology of the Supernatural	34
Two 'Eerie' Fairy Tales	35
Selkies and Mermaids: Fables of Love and Ecology	41
Postscript: when the Supernatural isn't the Supernatural	43
Ballad Women: Female Singers, Characters and Stories	45
Voices and Singers	45
Maidens, Temptresses, Heroines, and Jealous Sisters	47
'Burd Ellen', or why true love can never be disguised	52
Conclusion	54

Appendix   **56**
Sir Walter Scott, Ballad Collections and Collectors   56
The 'Literary Ballad' in Scotland   58
Broadside Ballads   60
Bothy Ballads   60

Bibliography   **62**
Ballad Recordings   65
Ballads on the internet   65

Notes   **66**

All the ballads discussed in this guide are taken from Emily Lyle's Canongate Classics edition, *Scottish Ballads* (1994; 2001), referenced by their number in that edition, and by stanza or line reference where appropriate.

List of ballads discussed or mentioned in alphabetical order
Bob Norris
Bog o' Gight
Bonny Barbara Allan
Burd Ellen
Clark Colven
Donald of the Isles
Earl Richard
Edom of Gordon
Edward, Edward
Gil Brenton
Hardyknute
Johnie Armstrang
Johnie Scott
Johnnie o' Braidiesleys
Johny Faa, the Gypsy Laddie
Katharine Jaffray
Kinmont Willie
Lady Maisry
Lamkin
Lord Jamie Douglas
Lord Lovat
Lord Ronald
Lord Thomas and Fair Annet
Lord Thomas and Fair Annie

Love Gregor
Marie Hamilton
Old Maitlan'
Sir Colin
Sir Patrick Spens
Son David
Sweet William's Ghost
Tam Lin
The Battle o' Harlaw
The Battle of Otterburn
The Bonny Earl of Murray
The Broomfield Hill
The Broom o' the Cathery Knowes
The Cruel Brother
The Cruel Mother
The Daemon Lover
The Douglas Tragedy
The Dowie Dens o' Yarrow
The Drowned Lovers
The Earl of Rosslyn's Daughter
The Farmer's Curst Wife
The Fause Knight
The Gaberlunzie-Man
The Gay Goss Hawk
The Gowans Sae Gay
The Great Silkie of Sule Skerry
The Jew's Daughter
The Laird o' Logie
The Maid of Coldingham
The Place Where My Love Johnny Dwells
The Shepherd's Dochter
The Thrie Ravens
The Twa Corbies
The Twa Magicians
The Twa Sisters
The Unco Knicht's Wouing
The Wife of Usher's Well
The Wind Hath Blown My Plaid Away
Thomas the Rhymer
Wee Messgrove
Young Bicham

SCOTNOTES

Study guides to major Scottish writers and literary texts

Produced by the Schools and Further Education Committee
of the Association for Scottish Literary Studies

Series Editors
Lorna Borrowman Smith
Ronald Renton

Editorial Board
Ronald Renton, St Aloysius' College, Glasgow
(Convener, Schools and Further Education Committee, ASLS)
William Aitken, Edinburgh
Jim Alison, HMI (retired)
Dr Eleanor Bell, University of Strathclyde
Dr Morna Fleming, Beath High School, Cowdenbeath
Professor Douglas Gifford, University of Glasgow
John Hodgart, Garnock Academy, Kilbirnie
Alan Keay, Portobello High School, Edinburgh
Alan MacGillivray, University of Strathclyde
Dr James McGonigal, University of Glasgow
Rev. Jan Mathieson, The Manse, Croy, Inverness
Lorna Ramsay, Fairlie, Ayrshire
Dr Kenneth Simpson, University of Strathclyde
Lorna Borrowman Smith, Stirling

THE ASSOCIATION FOR SCOTTISH LITERARY STUDIES aims to promote the study, teaching and writing of Scottish literature, and to further the study of the languages of Scotland.

To these ends, the ASLS publishes works of Scottish literature; literary criticism and in-depth reviews of Scottish books in *Scottish Studies Review*; short articles, features and news in *ScotLit*; and scholarly studies of language in *Scottish Language*. It also publishes *New Writing Scotland*, an annual anthology of new poetry, drama and short fiction, in Scots, English and Gaelic. ASLS has also prepared a range of teaching materials covering Scottish language and literature for use in schools.

All the above publications are available as a single 'package', in return for an annual subscription. Enquiries should be sent to: ASLS, c/o Department of Scottish History, 9 University Gardens, University of Glasgow, Glasgow G12 8QH. Telephone/fax +44 (0)141 330 5309, e-mail office@asls.org.uk or visit our website at **www.asls.org.uk**

EDITOR'S FOREWORD

The *Scotnotes* booklets are a series of study guides to major Scottish writers and literary texts that are likely to be elements within literature courses. They are aimed at senior pupils in secondary schools and students in further education colleges and colleges of education. Each booklet in the series is written by a person who is not only an authority on the particular writer or text but also experienced in teaching at the relevant levels in schools or colleges. Furthermore, the editorial board, composed of members of the Schools and Further Education Committee of the Association for Scottish Literary Studies, considers the suitability of each booklet for the students in question.

For many years there has been a shortage of readily accessible critical notes for the general student of Scottish literature. *Scotnotes* has grown as a series to meet this need, and provides students with valuable aids to the understanding and appreciation of the key writers and major texts within the Scottish literary tradition.

Lorna Borrowman Smith
Ronald Renton

Prelude

The Debateable Lands of the Ballads
'Ballads are awkward things...' In his classic account of the North-East ballad tradition, David Buchan (1939–94) made this seemingly extraordinary confession.[1] Beautiful, sad, strange, or comic, one might choose as adjectives to describe the Scottish ballads, but 'awkward'? In fact, ballads *do* present a particular kind of awkwardness to anyone seeking to study this vast inheritance of song from all corners of Scotland. It resides in what we might call their indeterminacy: ballads are now contested territory, being the disputed 'property' of folksingers and musicians, folklorists, historians, social anthropologists, social ethnologists, and last, but by no means least, literary critics. In truth, of course, the ballads 'belong' to no-one but the time and place and people who first share in their creation and to subsequent generations of ballad singers and audiences. This guide acknowledges the widely held view that ballads should not, and cannot, be studied as literary texts (some ballad-lovers contend that they should not be subject to analysis at all). But it hopes to suggest that the very contested nature of ballads allows them to raise interesting, unusual questions about the nature of interpretation and understanding which is illuminating for those who read and study literature. It might be suggested that their 'literariness', however controversial that notion seems to some ballad scholars, is their most neglected aspect. Though musicologists and other ballad critics may flinch at the way in which this guide explores in part what ballads can teach us about the nature of *reading,* of interpreting words and language, ballad 'awkwardness' can actually be viewed as a productive stirring of the critical, or cultural, pot.

Across the Threshold
A useful way to begin thinking about ballads is through the idea of *liminality*, a word derived from the Latin noun, *limen,* which means a threshold or doorway. Accordingly, a liminal state is one characterised by an intermediate or borderline quality; it is neither fully one thing nor another but resides in what the ballads themselves describe as a 'bateable [debateable] land'.

> And as we crossed the Bateable Land,
>   When to the English side we held
> The first o' men that we met wi,
>   Whae sould it be but fause Sakelde! (Lyle 2, st 20)

This verse is from the ballad 'Kinmont Willie', one of the most well-known of the 'Border Ballads'. The somewhat fearful speaker (after all, this is a border-crossing between England and Scotland in 1596) is here describing the grey area or shadowy land between the two nations. This disputed territory, belonging to neither country, figures in many other ballads (e.g. 'Katharine Jaffray', Lyle 24); it illustrates a geographically liminal ballad space. But ballads contain other types of liminality: the border between this world and the next is often seen to be porous, allowing for a two-way traffic between the living and the fairy world, as well as between the living and the dead. As well as forming part of the ballads' subject matter, the idea of liminality helpfully describes some of the ambiguity, outlined above, surrounding their status and interpretation. 'Liminality' can also be used as a critical tool to explain how the ballads cross traditional disciplinary boundaries and borders: they belong neither fully to the world of literature nor music but inhabit both. We should view ballad liminality as a positive feature, enriching and opening up, rather than limiting and prohibiting, our responses to, and enjoyment of, these multilayered, multidimensional forms.

Even if ballads aren't wholly the 'awkward things' we first believe them to be, they still remain elusive: resistant, like the proverbial butterfly, to being pinned down to a fixed form (there is no single, 'correct' version of any ballad, as we shall discover) or to a fixed meaning (what 'Thomas the Rhymer' 'means', for example, has been variously disputed). This is a good thing. But the experience of hearing a ballad sung, which is the original and traditional means of encountering the form, is not at all 'elusive'. Listening to a ballad singer can be an extraordinarily immediate and emotional experience, whatever the nature of the tale being told. And, at heart, a ballad is a story; and storytelling is the most ancient and traditional of 'literary' arts. Like all good stories, the power of the best traditional ballads rests on that vital connection between singer (or 'teller') and listener (or 'reader', we might add); that power to conjure up the enchanted fairy world of 'Tam Lin'; the ever-rising sea which buries Sir Patrick Spens and the Scottish sailors 'fifty fathoms deep' off the coast (Lyle 6, st 26); or the cackling conversation of the 'twa corbies' which wait, unmoved, for the wind to 'blaw for evermair' through the 'white banes, when they are bare' of a once-handsome knight (Lyle 82, st 5). Ballad stories speak about fundamental human emotions and predicaments, and so they are popular forms. As the writer Willa Muir puts it, they are 'felt in the blood and felt along the heart'.[2]

*

This study guide introduces the ways in which ballads, composed in Scots and English (therefore excluding the Gaelic song traditions), differ from what we conventionally think of as literary texts and how that influences our approach to, and experience of, the form. Ballad form and structure are explored in detail, as are the means by which ballads actually tell or 'narrate' their stories. This section concludes with a discussion of ballad language: its reliance on the power of imagery, metaphor and symbolism to convey meaning. Three key ballad themes or features are then explored in depth: the importance of history (how, and why, ballads dramatise significant historical events in the nation's life, and the lives of individual people and communities); the function of the supernatural (how, and why, do Scottish ballad traditions so markedly explore the realms of the 'otherworldly', whether they be inhabited by ghosts, fairies or magical creatures?); and, finally, the role of women, both as important ballad-tradition bearers and as ballad protagonists or characters who compel our attention, dramatically and psychologically. The Appendix contains brief notes on the history of ballad collecting, and on several further types of ballad, including the broadside and bothy traditions.

Introduction

What is a Ballad?
Broad definitions are helpful but necessarily limited, especially so in the case of the ballads; ballads have long been a part of traditional and popular culture in many societies, not simply Scotland. In fact, there is disagreement about where the term 'ballad' actually comes from. Some critics argue that the word, 'ballad' is derived from the Latin and Italian *ballare*, meaning to dance; a ballad might originally have denoted song or music to accompany a dance (dance-songs in late medieval literature were sometimes known as 'ballets'). Some ballad scholars even argue that the ballad form resists definition since 'among those who composed, sang or listened to it [...] there was no such concept'.[3] For now, although a ballad is first and foremost a *song*, it is helpful to think of the ballads' most typical features in terms of a literary *type* or *genre* that has a recognisable cluster of formal and thematic features which broadly persist, even when historical and geographical variation is taken into account. Put simply, the ballad is a folksong, a sung story which varies significantly in length but has a recognisable set of formal and thematic features.

Ballads, of course, are not unique to Scotland but are found as song types in popular, folk cultures across the world: for example, in Denmark from as early as the mid-twelfth century; in Germany and Spain from the fourteenth; in the Baltic and Slavonic countries from the fifteenth century. Rarely is any artistic form so diverse as the ballad form that it is found both in ancient Chinese literature and the folksongs of the southern Appalachian Mountains. But each tradition and culture has certain defining features. The Scottish ballad tradition is especially rich in songs of a romantic and tragic nature, in tales of the supernatural and in historical narratives. In particular, the Scottish ballad tradition is often defined by geographical region. Two of the most well known and popular are the so-called Border Ballads and the ballad tradition of the North-East, in particular Aberdeenshire. Geographical provenance is significant in many ways, not least because it can determine the songs' particular language register or dialect (as does historical period too), as well as being expressive of a local community and its culture: 'ballads come to be the completest definition of the community which enjoys them'.[4] Now that we have a basic working definition of ballads, we should consider how best to approach them.

Encountering the Ballads: different experiences

In this guide, all the ballads discussed are found in the most accessible anthology of ballads currently in print, the Canongate edition, edited by the distinguished ballad scholar Emily Lyle. Lyle's edition presents a wide-ranging choice of songs; but the ballad repertoire is vast and, unfortunately, we shall have to confine ourselves to Lyle's representative fragment. This helps focus our discussion but it is also important to be aware of other important collections. The standard edition is the monumental collection of ballads gathered and published by the scholar Professor Francis James Child in five volumes as *The English and Scottish Popular Ballads* (1882–98), comprising 305 ballads in around 1,000 versions. (You will find most critics identify a ballad by its number in Child.) However, the *least* traditional way to experience ballads is by reading them.

Ballads and Music

In using Lyle, or any other edition, we encounter ballads upon the page, coming to them as solitary readers. This is certainly not the way ballads were originally designed to be experienced! Ballads are songs; a singer and an audience (a family group, a social gathering, a farmhouse, a fair, a wedding – these and other communities comprised the traditional ballad audience) is the original context. Ideally, you should hear ballads sung. There are ceilidhs, folk festivals and other traditional song performances which offer the experience of ballads in a shared, communal context. There are also excellent recordings available of famous traditional singers, such as Bella Higgins, Jeannie Robertson and Duncan MacPhee, as well as contemporary folk reworkings and 'resettings' of traditional ballads (see the discography at the end). Listening to a combination of all these sources enriches appreciation and understanding both of the ballads themselves and of the different ways in which we respond, as listeners and readers. Although some of these experiences may seem more 'authentic' or 'true' than others, the notion of 'authenticity' itself is a fairly bogus one. We cannot be sure that a contemporary singer is communicating a given ballad to us in the way that it was first sung. Inevitably, our experiences of folksongs are different from those for whom they were first composed.

The very fact that we acknowledge our distance from songs that were heard originally in a wide range of social and cultural contexts makes us more imaginative and sympathetic respondents to ballads. It is vital to remember that the emotional and affective power of any ballad is twofold, derived from a composite of both words and melody. In this study, we are broadly concerned with only one 'half' of this fundamental unity. But tunes for the ballads discussed here can readily be found in the monumental collection edited by Bertrand Harris Bronson, *The Traditional Tunes of the Child Ballads*. His own abridged version, *The Singing Tradition of Child's Popular Ballads*, offers helpful and important insights into what he terms 'the vitalising, breath giving half of balladry'.[5] The interaction between words and melody determines the rhythmic flow, syntactical structure and phrasing of individual lines; words accommodate and bend to the organic patterning of the tune (particular tunes can exist in various forms, depending on when, where and by whom they were first recorded or transcribed). Individual singers choose to emphasise particular words or phrases, patternings or intonations (as simple and powerful as a falling or rising of the voice at the end of a line). A singer's voice can overturn or metamorphose our understanding into something very different from what a solitary, internal reading can achieve because no two singers perform a single ballad identically. The particular colouring of a singer's voice – its warmth, tonal qualities, accent or dialect, or age – matters greatly. Some ballad performers interweave song with spoken verse; the fusion of sung and spoken words creates its own distinct effects.

Do Ballads have 'Authors'?
The simple answer to this frequently asked question is no. The typical ballad exists in many different versions which are frequently not attributable to a single person. Often, the only ballad version that can be dated is the one first published, and *that* text is usually based on a long inheritance, transmitted by one generation of singers to another. This is usually referred to as the process of *oral transmission*. We shall return to this notion of ballad *orality*, but for now note that the typical ballad does not have a single, authoritative text or even a single, authoritative author. We usually believe that a creative artist (a writer, a painter, a composer) creates their work with some intention or meaning in mind, and that we, who read, look at or hear that work, must work out what it is. By contrast, traditional ballads rarely have an identifiable author, a single person to whom we can attribute a set of ideas or feelings that can then shape our understanding of the work. In practical terms, this does not matter; when we hear a ballad, the story is what is most

important. Ballad singers usually prefer to attribute their ballad to a particular singer from whom they learnt it. Yet, if ballads don't usually have a single *creator*, as a tradition they have a particular kind of *creativity*, or creative origin. Ballad scholars sometimes refer to theories of ballad composition known as the *individualist* and the *communalist*.

The individualist theory argues that any ballad must be the creation of one singer. This exists as the original and, by implication, 'best' version; subsequent renderings represent a kind of 'falling away'. The communalist theory, on the other hand, believes that any ballad is communally created, a creation shared amongst a community of singers, and remembered through generations of singers (this is sometimes referred to as *memorial transmission*). There is no single, 'ideal' version of a ballad but many co-existing and interrelated versions which all illustrate the *recreative* process of ballad-making. This is, perhaps, the most important point. Every new version of a ballad *recreates*, or *remakes*, the inherited story (in either a relatively 'minor' way, altering a word here and there; or more substantially, changing the story itself). Not only that but each and every time a ballad is sung, it is recreated. Singers recreate or *recompose* a ballad on every performance. Oral transmission, based on change and transformation, suggests a dynamic, constantly evolving kind of creativity. The tragic ballad of 'Lord Lovat', for example, was sung by the great modern folksinger Jeannie Robertson (1907–75) as a lullaby! Its gentle melody, rather than its intrinsic meaning, enabled this song thus to 're-emerge'. Whether we think ballads come into the world via communalist or individualist creation (or a mixture of both), the fact remains that we must jettison our common-sense notions of a fixed and unchanging literary text. If ballads themselves are always evolving, creative shape-shifters, if you like, then we, their audience, grow more receptive to the many different meanings they can yield.

Defining the Indefinable: the Ballad 'Text'

Another aspect of our encounter with ballads which runs contrary to contemporary expectations about how and what we read is that the texts in Lyle's edition are 'versions' of ballads; the texts we find there are not 'definitive' or final. There is no such thing as a definitive ballad text for, in short, there are as many variations of a ballad as there were (or are) singers. Most traditional singers learn ballads from other singers, and not 'from the page', as it were. And the controversy about whether ballads are to be considered as literature or not is revisited in the debate about whether ballads should even be printed or published. This, in fact, is an old complaint. To make a 'living', musical, oral form bend to the apparently fixed conventions of literature has long been felt to be artificial and unjust. Yet if editions and texts of ballads had not been published, they might have disappeared altogether. The most judicious way forward is to acknowledge these debates and dilemmas, to chart a balanced path through scholarly editions, and archival and contemporary recordings of songs, and to try to gain the 'lived' experience of hearing a ballad singer.

In conclusion, ballads are both like and unlike what we conventionally call 'literature'. This study guide will help you to analyse how a ballad is 'made' and how it communicates meaning; to discover the principal themes of the ballad tradition; and to appreciate the ways in which their forms and themes intersect with other literary and cultural traditions such as myth and fairy tale. This helps to explain why the ballads exert such a hold on our imaginations. Ballads occupy a very important place within Scottish culture. Because the roots of individual ballads can be old (some originate in the medieval period, though, as we shall see, it is often impossible to date ballads), they function as a kind of historical testimony. Ballad stories tell us about earlier historical periods in Scottish culture, and about the people and communities which made and listened to them from generation to generation. And all the while, we should not lose sight of what Jeannie Robertson sought to do: in learning the songs, to 'make them live'.[6]

Ballad Form, Structure and Style

The 'fluidity' of any ballad – the way in which it is a composite of words and melody created anew on each performance and each act of listening – should not diminish the importance of form, structure and technique. The great Skye poet Sorley MacLean (1911–96) memorably wrote about the quality of 'reticence' which he thought characterised Gaelic song and traditional Lowland Scots poetry. Consider, for example, the way in which the ship of 'Sir Patrick Spens' (Lyle 6) gradually sinks 'across' these two verses. The language of the second stanza closely mirrors the first, with the exception of the final line, where delicate variation (the substitution of 'still' for 'letna') signals hopelessness. Simple, 'unshowy', but nevertheless powerful, it aptly illustrates ballad 'reticence':

> 'Gae fetch a web o' the silken claith,
>   Another o' the twine
> And wap them into our ship's side,
>   And letna the sea come in.'
>
> They fetched a web o' the silken claith,
>   Another o' the twine,
> And they wrapped them roun that gude ship's side,
>   But still the sea came in. (st 19–20)

The qualities which MacLean perceived as 'intense emotion', the 'simple intensity' of form and 'sheer economy of word', are largely a consequence of the interplay between ballad structure, style and language choice.

The Ballad Stanza

Unlike modern poetry, which is often written in a 'free lyric style' (not shaped by fixed rhyme and metre), the traditional ballad is composed within a specific verse pattern. This is usually referred to as the 'ballad stanza'. It consists of four lines (a *quatrain*) where the rhyme scheme is usually *abcb*, as in:

> O hooly, hooly rose she up,
>   To the place where he was lying,
> And when she drew the curtain by,
>   'Young man, I think you're dying.'
>   ('Bonny Barbara Allan', Lyle 79, st 3)

Occasionally the rhyme scheme may vary in a single ballad, as in the ballad 'The Jew's Daughter' (Lyle 73), where a few stanzas rhyme *abab:*

> And scho has taine out a little pen-knife,
>   And low down by her gair;
> Scho has twin'd the yong thing and his life,
>   A word he nevir spak mair. (st 4)

As well as rhyme, another 'sound-pattern' is created by *stress* (the emphasis placed on a syllable, or unit of sound). In the ballad stanza, four beats (stresses) in one line alternate with three beats (stresses) in the next. So:

> They hadna been a week, a week
>   In Noroway but twae...
>   ('Sir Patrick Spens', Lyle 6, st 9)

The pattern formed by these stressed and unstressed syllables (a four-three-four-three stress pattern) helps to create the *metre*. This can be defined as the overall pattern of stressed and unstressed syllables in a line. In ballad poetry, this pattern usually conforms to the *iamb*: an unstressed syllable followed by a stressed syllable. For example:

> Lord John stood in his stable-door
>   Said he was bound to ride;
> Burd Ellen stood in her bowr-door,
>   Said she'd rin by his side. ('Burd Ellen', Lyle 20, st 3)

Although the metre provides a fixed rhythmic stress pattern, it works in tandem with the musicality of a singer's voice, which may manipulate the flow of stress and emphasis differently; this, combined with the role of ballad music itself, makes room for flexibility and variation.

Ballad Patterns
(1) Repetition
Almost all poetry depends on a particular patterning, or arrangement, of words and sounds which helps to create both rhythm and other kinds of *aural* (heard) schemes, as in medieval Scottish poetry where a single poetic line may be bound cohesively

by the device of alliteration ('I haue ane wallidrag, ane worme, ane auld wobat carle'), or in the extraordinary sound patterns of the poet Gerard Manley Hopkins ('A windpuff-bonnet of fawn-froth / Turns and twindles over the broth').[7] One simple patterning device in the ballads, influencing rhythm and sound, is repetition. Repetitive patterns enable a song to be more easily remembered, and also allow an audience to join in with the singer at naturally anticipated moments. Repetition of a word (or words) can occur within a single line, as here in 'The Battle of Otterburn' (Lyle 1): 'But I have *dreamd* a dreary *dream*...' (st 19, repeated st 24); or in a single stanza as in the binary pattern of this verse from 'Bonny Barbara Allan': 'And *slowly, slowly* raise she up, / And *slowly, slowly* left him' (Lyle 79, st 7). Repetition may also include the recurrence of a certain phrase within a ballad; for example, in 'Sweet William's Ghost' (Lyle 30), the phrase 'faith and troth' (stanzas 4, 5, 7, 8, 10) is important in a song which explores the idea of love after death; or of a phrase which describes a gesture, as in this stanza from 'Sir Colin' (Lyle 38): '*He gae* her rings to her fingers, / Sae did he ribbons to her hair; / *He gae* her a broach to her briest-bane, / For fear that they sud neer meet mair' (st 10).

In the ballads, as in folk tradition, fairy tales and medieval literature, numbers (and periods of time) have a special significance, and their importance is often highlighted by repetition: 'They hadna been *a week* from her, / *A week* but barely ane, / When word came to the carline wife / That her three sons were gane' ('The Wife of Usher's Well', Lyle 31, st 2); 'There were *five and five* before them a' / Wi hunting-horns and bugles bright; / And *five and five* came wi Buccleuch, / Like Warden's men, arrayed for fight' ('Kinmont Willie', Lyle 2, st 18).

Another instance of repetition in the ballads is through the question and answer device. Dialogue, as we shall see when exploring ballad narration, is a popular device: either as an exchange between characters, or simply as an exchange between two 'voices', the narrator's and another interlocutor.

(1)
O, did ye fae the Heilans come,
  Or did ye come that wye?
Or did ye see Macdonal's men,
  As they came fae the Skye?

> O yes, me fae the Hielans cam,
>   And me cam a' the wye,
> And I did see the Macdonal's men,
>   As they cam fae the Skye.
>   ('The Battle o' Harlaw', Lyle 4, st 3–4)

(2)
> 'But wha will bake my bridal bread,
>   Or brew my bridal ale?
> And wha will welcome my brisk bride,
>   That I bring oer the dale?'
>
> 'It's I will bake your bridal bread,
>   And brew your bridal ale,
> And I will welcome your brisk bride,
>   That you bring oer the dale'
>   ('Lord Thomas and Fair Annie', Lyle 25, st 2–3)

The popularity of the question and answer dialogue partly reflects the oral, communal context of ballad creation; an audience can easily join in these exchanges. The repetition of certain words or phrases also makes the ballad easier to remember (as it is in children's nursery rhymes) and is called a *mnemonic* device. Not only is it a practical device but it influences the 'mood' and 'tone' of a ballad, helping to create its emotional and psychological world.

Ballad scholars sometimes refer to the process of *incremental repetition*: the same phrase is repeated with progressive variations throughout a song. Despite its apparent simplicity, repetition is extraordinarily effective:

> And he has burnd the dales of Tyne,
>   And part of Bambrough shire,
> And three good towers on Reidswire fells,
>   He left them all on fire.
>
> And he marchd up to Newcastle,
>   And rode it round about:
> 'O wha's the lord of this castle?
>   Or wha's the lady o't?'

In these two stanzas, from the opening of the 'The Battle of Otterburn' (Lyle 1, st 3–4), the repetition is simple: the conjunction 'and' is repeated at the beginning of five of the eight lines. This certainly makes them memorable; but the stylistic device also creates more abstract effects. Given that this ballad is about war and conflict, what better way to convey the successful invasion of the 'doughty Douglas' and his men into the North of England than by thus linking together their destructive enterprises? Tension is created as the outcome of battle becomes clear.

The narrator of 'The Douglas Tragedy' (Lyle 61) enigmatically concludes the tale of Lord William and Lady Margret, 'true lovers' who are only united in death, by saying:

> *And* they *twa* met, and they *twa* plat,
>   *And* fain they wad be near;
> *And* a' the warld might ken right weel
>   They were *twa* lovers dear. (st 19)

Just as the lovers themselves become entwined in one another ('plat': 'pleated together', like the rose and the briar which grow out of their graves), so their tragic fates are bound up in the interlinking 'and' of this last verse, and somehow perfectly inevitable.

In the closing stanzas of 'Edom of Gordon' (Lyle 8), verbal repetition also evokes urgency, but here, the stress pattern created by emphasis on 'mony' (many) makes for a desolate poignancy:

> But *mony* were the mudie men
>   Lay gasping on the grien;
> For o' fifty men that Edom brought out
>   There were but five ged heme.
>
> And *mony* were the mudie men
>   Lay gasping on the grien,
> And *mony* were the fair ladys
>   Lay lemanless at heme. (st 27–8)

This reference to the innumerable fallen men, and the women who mourn them, seems like a chant, or incantation, heightened by the alliteration at work within these lines (/m/, /g/, /l/). Such rhythmic incantation is often the effect of repetition: 'Oh I'm *gaun awa* in a *bottomless boat*, / In a *bottomless boat*, in a *bottomless boat*, / For I'm *gaun awa* in a *bottomless boat*, / An I'll never return again' ('Son David', Lyle 66, st 9).

(2) The Ballad Formula

You may have observed how frequently certain phrases seem to recur in the ballads, such as 'milk-white', an epithet used variously to describe female beauty, clothing or animals, as in 'I'll gie thee all these milk-whyt steids' ('Johnie Armstrang', Lyle 3, st 10). Such phrases are known as *ballad formulas* (or *formulae*). A ballad formula refers to a fixed unit of words, a set verbal pattern (sometimes referred to as a *prefabricated linguistic unit*) which can be 'picked up' and used in different ballad contexts by a singer who senses intuitively what formula is most suitable for a particular moment. *Formulaic* phrases are not unique to ballad composition but are found in many forms of traditional, largely oral poetry. These formulaic phrases are sometimes used to fill a line, or inserted for a rhythmic purpose, or to offer the singer respite from the 'burden' of memory recall. Some examples of formulaic phrases, and their subtle variants, are:

(1)
He leaned his back against an oak
('Johnnie o' Braidiesleys', Lyle 5, st 13)

She's leand her back against the wa
('Burd Ellen', Lyle 20, st 30)

She's set her back untill a tree
('The Cruel Mother', Lyle 74, st 4)

(2)
Ride up, ride up ...
('The Cruel Brother', Lyle 65, st 12 and 13)
Won up, won up, Lizie Lindsay ...
('Donald of the Isles', Lyle 12, st 23)

As well as helping the action of the story along, ballad formulas also fulfil what has been termed a *supra-narrative function*. The Latin prefix, *supra*, means 'above' or 'transcending', so the 'supra-narrative' function refers to any device which creates an effect beyond the 'bare', literal events of the story. Alternatively, one might say that ballad formulas, which vary from being a phrase, a line or a stanza, have a 'connotative' function: they imply or suggest something in addition to what is explicitly stated. For example, the recurrent phrase, 'He's taen her by the milk white hand', usually referring to a knight, elf or spirit leading a young maiden, usually acts as a portent of sexual union, whether tender or violent. Our ability to recognise certain formulas enables us to anticipate the next stage of the ballad drama. Far from being equated with clichéd or stereotypical expression, they actually fulfil a creative function in making the audience search for associations and meaning. They also fulfil our need for the pleasure of familiarity and recognition. Ballads often wrestle with the 'big themes' (appropriately, they are sometimes referred to as the *muckle* [big] *sangs*) – the fundamental human life-experiences of love, loss and death – so it is appropriate that part of the vocabulary with which they do so has a familiar, repetitive, and almost mythical resonance.

Ballad Narration and Storytelling
If the telling of a 'good story' is the heart of ballad tradition, we must consider how, and by what means, its tales are told: in other words, just how a ballad is *narrated*. Initially, we might suggest that narration is an 'intuitive' process, relying on the instinctive skill and knowledge of ballad storytellers who do not have a 'methodology' but let the song unfold 'through' them. But their creativity is many-sided. Like all traditional storytellers, the ballad singer is in an interesting position as part inheritor of tradition and part innovator. Ballad narration combines a constant (traditional storytelling patterns, familiar from folktales, myths, fairy tales and other types) with a variable (the distinctive style, mood and emphasis of an individual singer).

(1) Popular Features of Ballad Storytelling and Style
While allowing for an individual teller's re-creation and variation, ballad scholars have identified a cluster of characteristics common to ballad narration.

(a) It is dramatic, usually beginning at the heart of the story, without any elaborate 'prologue' or introduction; similarly, it ends abruptly. Good examples of openings which drop us straight into the heart of the story are 'The Unco Knicht's Wouing' (Lyle 17): 'There was a Knight ridin' frae the East' (st 1) and, very dramatically, 'Son David' (Lyle 66): 'Oh, what's the blood 'it's on your sword ...' (st 1). On the other hand, some ballads allude to place and time, though often elusively like the 'Once upon a time' opening of a fairy tale, such as 'The Battle of Otterburn' (Lyle 1): 'It fell about the Lammas tide', or 'Edom of Gordon': 'It fell about the Martinmas' (Lyle 8). Depending on the kind of story they tell, many ballads end starkly or suddenly, such as 'Sweet William's Ghost' (Lyle 30): 'Wan grew her cheeks, she closd her een, / Stretchd her soft limbs, and dy'd' (st 16). Some songs leave their ending rather 'open', eschewing the finality of what literary critics sometimes call 'narrative closure', such as 'The Broom o' the Cathery Knowes' (Lyle 64): 'Have you any gold, my true-love?' she says, / 'Or have you any fee? / Or have you come to see your own love hanged, / Like a dog, upon a tree?' (st 14). 'The Battle o' Harlaw' (Lyle 4) ends not abruptly but with a sense of sad, almost ironic reflection at what has happened: 'If anyone did ask you, / Where's the men you had awa? / Ye may tell him plain and very plain, / They're sleepin at Harlaw' (Lyle 4).

(b) It is 'impersonal' in its narration; in other words, there is no trace of the ballad maker's 'personality' or thoughts, nor does the singer impose any comment or judgement on its characters and events. Questions of feeling, whether emotional or moral, are entirely left to us, the audience; the ballad world itself refuses to be drawn on this account. However, we might make a distinction between the ballad singer or teller (the 'actual person' narrating the tale), and the 'narrator' or narrative voice we hear within the ballad. In other words, the ballad singer may be adopting or performing in a different 'voice'; for example, 'Lord Jamie Douglas' (Lyle 46) is spoken in the first-person voice of the young woman, Lord Jamie's lover. And occasionally, we *are* made aware of the storyteller: 'Of a gentleman I sing a sang' ('Johnie Armstrang', Lyle 3, st 1); and even of his or her function as a witness as in 'The Battle o' Harlaw' (Lyle 4): 'As I cam in the Geerie lan's / And in by Netherha', / I saw sixty thoosan redcoats ...' (st 1). And if a ballad refers to 'our' and 'we' in the course of its telling, as in 'Johny Faa, the Gypsy Laddie' (Lyle 13), then its story becomes a shared and inclusive experience.

(c) Ballad narrative often proceeds, or is driven onwards, by the use of ballad 'formulae', as we have seen, which can also influence mood and tone. Such transitions from, or links between, episodes means that the story unfolds swiftly.

(d) Emphasis is placed on the dramatic situation itself ('the story'), on action and dialogue, and much less on other features, such as continuity of narrative or characterisation, usually portrayed by a minimum of detail and descriptive setting. Any descriptive detail which *is* found therefore usually serves a purpose but ballad-makers are not *entirely* averse to embellishment; for example, in 'Sir Patrick Spens' (Lyle 6, st 25), the reference to the 'goud kaims' in the hair of the 'maidens' who mourn their drowned lovers is an important visual detail, crystallising their wealth and beauty which now seems frail and inadequate against the enormity of death and loss.

(2) Characterisation
Powerful and memorable characters can be found in the ballads, such as Janet, the famous heroine of 'Tam Lin' (see later), but in general 'character' in the ballad world is very different from the idea of 'character' familiar from other literary modes such as the modern novel; in other words, people with fully fledged consciousnesses, or identifiable 'personalities'. We rarely have access to the interior world of ballad characters: their thoughts and feelings. Rather than expecting the highly developed explorations of character we find in modern novels, it might be more useful to think of ballads as sharing with folk and fairy tales characters who are recognisable 'types': the wicked stepmother, the good younger daughter. The distinguished Russian scholar Vladimir Propp (1895–1970), when analysing the narrative structure of folktales or 'wonder tales' (*Zaubermärchen*) noted that in these story-types 'functions of characters serve as stable, constant elements in a tale, independent of how and by whom they are fulfilled. They constitute the fundamental components of a tale'.[8] He argued that the 'names of the *dramatis personae* change (as well as the attributes of each), but neither their actions nor functions change'.[9] What he means is that individual personality traits are of little importance; the *dramatis personae* of a tale always represent unchanging general types such as (according to Propp) the hero, the villain, a young girl (and her father), the helper, the dispatcher, a magical character. This is because, according to Propp, traditional stories tend to portray 'situations which repeat themselves and are transferable'.[10]

This also holds true of story patterning and, accordingly, characterisation in traditional ballads. A similar list of character types might be drawn up for the ballads who share similar features (and storytelling functions), though their names may differ: for example, the young girl, usually from the peasant class; the aristocratic lady; the courtly knight; the warrior-hero; the shepherd boy and girl; the mother figure. Usually, these character types have particular positive or negative features.

Ultimately, although Propp's theory helps us to appreciate the story patterns of ballad tale types and characters in particular, it does not deny us the capacity to respond *emotionally* to them. The fact that the young 'layde' who 'lived in the North, / ... called Sara' in 'The Dowie Dens o' Yarrow' (Lyle 60, st 1) may illustrate the general character type of the young girl wronged in love, and the tale itself exemplify some of Propp's 'functions', does not stop us from feeling moved by her plight (her brother has killed her lover). Willa Muir has an interesting phrase to describe the ballads' slow, sure hold upon our emotions: she refers to their 'underworld of feeling'.[11] So the popular assumption that ballad characterisation is somehow psychologically crude because the characters are simply general types should be qualified because a good ballad has the power to make its characters 'live'. What we can more justly conclude is that ballad figures are often imagined in *archetypal* terms (the noun 'archetype' comes from a Greek word, meaning 'original pattern'): characters who are recognisable, indeed universal, types because their fate illustrates the archetypal themes and motifs which preoccupy the ballads – rites of passage, love, death, the arduous quest, vengeance and betrayal, the successful undertaking of difficult tasks. Later, we shall explore how archetypes interact with particular psychological, moral and social forces in the depiction of female characters.

(3) Ballad Language: Image and Symbol

So far we have considered how ballad makers use formal devices such as repetition and formulae, and how recognition of these popular features heightens our appreciation of the songs. Yet, though the pleasure of ballads partly lies in the familiarity of these devices, and their role in unfolding 'the ballad drama', equal pleasure comes from the *instability* of ballad meaning. This means that however much 'stability' or fixity of meaning (such as formulae or universal narrative patterning) is crucial to our experiences of the ballads, the power of the unexpected and arresting phrase is also important, such as this deeply enigmatic verse from 'Thomas the Rhymer':

> O they rade on, and farther on,
>   And they waded thro rivers aboon the knee,
> And they saw neither sun nor moon,
>   But they heard the roaring of the sea. (Lyle 36, st 15)

or this omen-laden description of lunar change in 'Sir Patrick Spens':

> 'I saw the new moon late yestreen,
>   Wi the auld moon in her arm ...' (Lyle 6, st 13)

Ballad language can cast meaning into flux, loosening its conventional fixity of meaning. Many ballads illustrate the possibility of what literary critics sometimes refer to as *polysemy*: 'the possibility of a simultaneous multiplicity of meaning encoded within a single phrase or text'. In other words, because we are unsure *exactly* what is being referred to, the ballad acquires a more suggestive or evocative power. We might borrow the idea of *estrangement* or *defamiliarisation* from the Russian literary critic Victor Shklovsky (1893–1984) to describe the poetic effect, and potential, of the most powerful ballad language. On the whole, ballads do not use, as other literary discourses do, a highly *figurative* language: that is, language which uses figures of speech such as metaphor and simile. Nevertheless, ballad language is often a highly *symbolic* language. A symbol is usually defined as a representation of something else, whether an idea, object or concept. In myth and literature, symbols serve as a kind of imaginative 'shorthand', distilled from an extraordinary variety of sources, to represent concepts and ideas: for example, the laurel tree may signify the art of poetry; the phoenix bird the idea of rebirth and resurrection. Ballads inherit their symbolism mostly from traditional folklore.

One of the most obvious illustrations of ballad symbolism is the use of colour. Not only do certain colours become absorbed within formulaic discourse, as we have already seen, but they constitute the ballads' most obvious visual and imaginative language. We find frequent allusions to green, as in:

> But she kilted up her green claithing
>   ('The Place Where My Love Johnny Dwells', Lyle 21, st 4)
>
> May Margaret has kilted her green cleiding
>   ('The Laird o' Logie', Lyle 53, st 4)
>
> Janet has kilted her green kirtle   ('Tam Lin', Lyle 35, st 3)
>
> He's taen her by the sleeve sae green
>   ('Clark Colven', Lyle 33, st 6)

> She has kilted her coats o' green silk
>> ('Donald of the Isles', Lyle 12, st 12)

Green, probably the most popular ballad colour, calls up a wealth of associations with nature, fertility, sexuality and, in addition, the fairy world; unsurprisingly, as the above examples show, it is most commonly associated with young women. Another symbolic colour reference in the ballad is 'milk-white' which frequently signifies female beauty, as in the formulaic 'milk-white hand'. The gaberlunzie man sings a song, beginning 'I wish says she I were as white, / As ever the Snow lay on the Dyke' ('The Gaberlunzie-Man', Lyle 11, st 3). The most beautiful and noble horses in the ballads are always 'milk-white' (cf. 'The Shepherd's Dochter', Lyle 43, st 5); and the horse on which Tam Lin rides out of fairy land is 'milk-white'. Other ballad colours include gold ('masts o' the beaten gold', 'The Daemon Lover', Lyle 19, st 9); and adorning the body of the drowned sister in 'The Twa Sisters' are 'gold and pearle', a 'gouden girdle' and 'gouden rings' (Lyle 29, st 20–2); yellow (as in conventionally beautiful 'yellow' (fair) hair, and the yellow flowers of the broom); and 'berry brown'. While these colours have certain associations or meanings, they are not *absolutely* fixed or precise. Those imaginatively visual and symbolic ballad worlds call upon *our* powers of imaginative responsiveness to unearth evocative and hidden meanings.

(4) The Language of Nature

Ballads may be set in a variety of 'worlds' or landscapes but the natural landscape is one of the most persistent and popular ballad settings, an offshoot both of the powerful creative influences of folklore and popular belief, and of the ballad propensity for symbolic language.

> Lord Barnard's awa to the green wood
>> ('Wee Messgrove', Lyle 26, st 1)

> Bob Norris is to the grein wud gane
>> ('Bob Norris', Lyle 27, st 1)
> ...An tell her to cum to the merrie grein wud (st 3)

> For to the greenwood I must gae
> To pu the nut but an the slae
>> ('Gil Brenton', Lyle 41, st 49)

In classical and medieval poetry, nature is often contrasted with the 'civilised', social world, representing freedom from its artificiality and constraints (we see this in Shakespeare's comedies and romances too). The ballads probably reflect this semi-mythical view of nature but specifically the 'green woods' of the ballads are places in which romantic and sexual liaisons take place (hence the colour green's association with sexuality and fertility!) and where the fairies, and other supernatural creatures, are generally to be located; as Willa Muir put it, the greenwood is 'an annexe to the archaic world'.[12] Specifically, flowers, plants and trees can have magical powers (in 'The Broomfield Hill', Lyle 40, yellow broom is believed magically to restore a girl's virginity; and the angry Fairy Queen in 'Tam Lin' appears 'out of a bush o' broom'), or assume symbolic significance, acting as a kind of metaphorical shorthand.

In 'The Douglas Tragedy' (Lyle 61), Lord William, who is killed by his beloved's brothers, and Lady Margret, who dies for love of him, are buried together 'in St Mary's kirk'. Only in the earth does their love survive: 'Out o' the lady's grave grew a bonny red rose, / And out o' the knight's a briar' (st 18). The symbolism of the two intertwined plants partly derives from the famous medieval legend of Tristan and Isolde's love. It can also be seen in 'The Thrie Ravens' (Lyle 83), where a 'fir' and a lily grow into a 'true love knot' that reaches the 'kirk top'. Certain trees have superstitious or magical associations, such as rowan, hawthorn and holly, as well as the archetypal biblical association, as in 'Thomas the Rhymer', of the tree of knowledge. The language of nature can be both pagan and Christian.

Nature's symbolic role in the ballads also extends to animals and birds; like medieval literature, and traditional myths and legends, ballads find supernatural or spiritual meaning in animals. Ballads also share the popular folkloric belief that fairies can take the shape of any bird or creature they wish (especially strong in Highland tradition); in that sense, animals can connect the human world to the 'other worlds' of the ballad. Generally, birds and animals have a positive role to play. In the startlingly violent ballad 'Lamkin' (Lyle 72), about the stonemason who takes revenge on the noble lord who does not pay his wages by murdering his baby and wife, birds bear witness to his execution and that of the nurse who helped him; their singing implies some final kind of harmony:

> O sweetly sang the black-bird
>   That sat upon the tree;
> But sairer grat Lamkin,
>   When he was condemnd to die.
>
> And bonny sang the mavis,
>   Out o' the thorny brake;
> But sairer grat the nourice,
>   When she was tied to the stake. (st 26–27)

Elsewhere birds have magical powers and can speak. Most famously, 'The Twa Corbies' (Lyle 82), printed in Scott's *Minstrelsy*, are two crows (large, hooded black birds that unsurprisingly have negative folkloric associations) who discuss how they intend to dine on the corpse of a 'new slain knight' (st 2). The gleeful description of how they shall devour his 'bonny blue een' (st 4) gruesomely mirrors their final reflection that the knight will not be missed or mourned; even his lady has found a new love. These birds crow over a desolate world of tarnished romance and lonely death. In the closely connected ballad 'The Thrie Ravens' (Lyle 83), the knight's body is attended by his faithful hounds and loyal, pregnant lady; still, the 'black as black' birds symbolise death. In 'Earl Richard' (Lyle 76), the jealous lady who has newly murdered a knight meets a 'wee bird on a tree' (st 14) who knows her crime; to her promise that she will keep him in a golden cage, he replies:

> 'Ye wad cut aff my little head
>   Throw my body in the sea
> An as ye said to your trew luve
>   Sa wad ye say to me' (st 17)

'Telland [telling] ill tales' about her, the bird flies to freedom in the forest.

The Drama of the Past:
Telling History through Ballads

The ballads explored in this section draw inspiration from the past, transmuting historical events and characters into vivid and compelling stories. Many of these ballads fulfil the traditional role of song and music in all cultures, playing a vital role in helping to express the shared thoughts and feelings of a community. Collective, 'lived' experiences can thereby be transmitted through ballad song, allowing singers and audiences to (re)experience or (re)imagine the past. A society may create and perpetuate songs which dramatise events, characters or experiences of particular significance; 'they are a commemoration, emotionally generated, of family and regional loyalties within the events the narratives portray'.[13] Certain historical experiences have become especially 'popular' or meaningful in Scottish song culture, such as the eighteenth-century Jacobite risings or, as in traditional ballads, the medieval border warfare between Scotland and England. Many ballads concern national loss or failure, or a tragic event of more local, particular significance; the fact that the historical events which are artistically remembered are not always 'positive' is an important part of their emotional power. Like the still flourishing genre of political protest song, ballads could be composed within a community to express disquiet or unease. Poetry and music, especially when combined, can enshrine cultural memory and social solidarity.

The historical ballads therefore offered people a way of comprehending the past; and they permit us to enter into the shadowlands of the past by rendering it vivid and immediate, and thereby more understandable. Characters may be historical (figures of national significance, such as Mary, Queen of Scots, or Bonnie Prince Charlie) or fictional. Ballads do not depict history in a conventional or straightforward manner: the story, rather than verifiable accuracy, is the thing, although Sir Walter Scott, ever the 'historical romancer', was careful to include copious historical notes and information in his collection. Bare historical fact metamorphoses into dramas of romance and violence. But however imaginatively free ballad history tales may be, they also express 'unrecorded experience'; that is, give voice to the people whose stories are usually unheard in mainstream historical records.

(i) Ballads at the Frontiers of War
(1) 'Kinmont Willie' (Lyle 2)
Our first example of the ballad history tradition is this song, first collected in Sir Walter Scott's *Minstrelsy* (see Appendix on Scott's ballad collection). It tells the particular story of one William Armstrong, 'known as Will of Kinmont', a 'bauld' (bold) sixteenth-century Border thief, who was captured by English troops and heroically rescued by the Laird of Buccleuch, with the aid of no less than several hundred Scotsmen, on 13 April 1596. Will's capture was felt keenly since a truce between Scotland and England had been drawn: in the song, Buccleuch magnanimously points out that 'since nae war's between the lands / ...I'll neither harm English lad or lass' (st 15). In contrast, the English troops' brutal seizure of Will, destined for execution, is vividly portrayed (note how repetition is used):

> They band his legs beneath the steed,
>   They tied his hands behind his back;
> They guarded him, fivesome on each side
>   And they brought him ower the Liddel-rack.
>
> They led him to the Liddel-rack,
>   And also thro the Carlisle sands;
> They brought him to Carlisle castell,
>   To be at my Lord Scroope's command. (st 3 and 4)

Will's undaunted spirit – 'My hands are tied, but my tongue is free' (st 5) – is paralleled by the furious words (and gesture) of 'the bauld Keeper' (Buccleuch): 'He has taen the table wi his hand, / He garrd the red wine spring on hie; / "Now Christ's curse on my head," he said, / "But avenged of Lord Scroop I'll be!" ' (st 9). Particular dramatic devices are used which help win our sympathies for, and allegiance to, Willie's cause: the narrative perspective is from the point of view of one of Buccleuch's men ('When to the English side we held, / The first o' men that we met wi...', st 20). Lengthy exchanges of dialogue occur across 'enemy lines': ' "Where be ye gaun, ye hunters keen?" / Quo fause Sakelde; "come tell to me!" / "We go to hunt an English stag, / Has trespassed on the Scots countrie"' (st 21). Such highly emotive language draws attention to the significance of land and territory; throughout this ballad, the borders and rivers of this 'bateable' region never lose their political charge. But Willie's rescue and escape on the wild horse, 'Red Rowan', is jubilantly, almost

The Scottish Ballads

riotously, portrayed: his 'airns playd clang' (st 39), so unbelievably fast does he ride. As the breathless narrative pace finally slows, his deliverer, Buccleuch, throws a final taunt to the 'astonished' English lord, left standing at the other side of Eden Water: ' "If ye like na my visit in merry England, / In fair Scotland come visit me!"' (st 44).

(2) 'The Battle o' Harlaw' (Lyle 4)
The celebratory, almost comic-book *brio* of 'Kinmont Willie', which delights in individual heroic courage and 'national' triumph, however small, contrasts with the mood and style of other historical ballads of warfare. 'The Battle o' Harlaw', dramatising the contest fought in 1411 between the forces of Donald of the Isles, and those of the Earl of Mar and the Sherriff of Angus, at Harlaw, north-west of Aberdeen, shows that there are no victors in any war. The sheer desolation and loss of young life on both sides (though the Highland army was particularly devastated) is powerfully evoked in the almost child-like, incantatory refrain: 'I saw sixty thoosan redcoats / A' marchin to Harlaw. / *Wi' my derry dey, dumpty dow, / A daddle um a dee*' (Lyle 4, st 1). The song is structured as a dialogue between the narrator and two witnesses to the battle. In the final verse, the soldiers who have been cut down 'as a scythe doth the green grass' (st 17) are imagined by a strangely gentle image, despite the tune's strong, robust melody: 'If anyone did ask at you, / Where's the men you had awa? / Ye may tell him plain and very plain, / They're sleepin at Harlaw' (st 26). The use of the present tense invests the act of historical retelling both with an immediacy and sense of timelessness, as though the fallen soldiers eternally lie 'asleep'.

(3) 'The Battle of Otterburn' (Lyle 1)
The war waged by Scottish and English forces against each other on 19 August 1388 is the subject of one of the most famous of Border ballads, 'The Battle of Otterburn'. The fight between the Scottish Earl Douglas, and the English Lord Percy, is told in bold heroic style – 'They swakked their swords, till sair they swat, / And the blood ran down like rain' (st 21) – with deference to medieval chivalric codes of honour: the defeated Percy eventually yields to the 'courteous knight', Montgomery. Yet although the ballad celebrates the Scottish victory, it is also deeply elegiac in tone: the fatally injured Douglas, who has already prophesied his own death (st 19), wants to die, unseen, 'by the braken-bush, / Beneath the blooming brier' (st 26). The song mourns a fallen hero

as much as it commemorates a Scottish victory. Its epic-style heroism is therefore qualified and muted by a more vulnerable portrayal of a romance-like hero. This impulse does not detract from the predominantly combative and martial spirit of this and other Border ballads of war and conflict; but by creating narratives which view that conflict from particular individuals' perspectives, the Border ballad makers rarely let us forget the 'humanity' behind historical and epoch-making events.

(ii) New Stories from Old Facts
Historical ballads may also be based on a single character or highly specific incident. The ballad 'Lord Jamie Douglas' (Lyle 46), for example, is a portrait of the broken marriage between Lady Barbara Erskine and James, Marquis of Douglas, from the former's point of view. The famous ballad 'The Bonny Earl of Murray' (Lyle 7) concerns the murder of the Protestant nobleman Lord James Stewart, Earl of Moray, by the Catholic Huntly family in 1592. In the fraught post-Reformation context of Renaissance Scotland, this caused considerable political and religious controversy; so much, in fact, that it becomes appropriate subject matter for a popular ballad. Moray is romantically portrayed, the epitome of courtly and chivalric love:

> He was a braw gallant,
>   And he playd at the glove;
> And the bonny Earl of Murray
>   Oh he was the Queen's love! (st 5)

This stylised presentation of Moray could hardly be called impartial! No doubt the ballad was designed to appeal to the sympathies and loyalty of the Protestant faction which supported Moray. That we can interpret an apparently 'simple' ballad in this politicised way (though we can also enjoy its story without such historical knowledge) demonstrates that ballads could be created to capture the mood of popular feeling and political sentiment. Though we cannot precisely date many 'historically themed' ballads (were they composed immediately after the event, or after a period of longer historical reflection?), they themselves are a part of history, a living fragment of the historical episode or process they seek to record. It is often in ballad form that pivotal historical events are transmitted to posterity and remembered; ballads help to create cultural memory – those inherited aspects of identity (national, communal, geographical; identity is multifaceted) that help us define who we are. The historical ballads have also been understood as 'a form of education', originally able to portray 'the political history' of region and place to a largely non-literate community.[14] And, as the song of the 'Earl of Murray' ballad shows, they seek to entertain and to provoke as well.

(iii) The Passions of History: 'Edom of Gordon'

David Buchan observes that though ballads cannot serve as straightforward historical 'documents' or 'evidence' they instead offer 'emotional truths'.[15] This eloquently describes 'Edom of Gordon' (Lyle 8). This ballad depicts the historical incident of the burning of Alexander Forbes's castle in Aberdeenshire in 1571 by Sir Adam Gordon (though in this version the scene is geographically moved south to Berwickshire; factual accuracy is not the most important point for ballad-makers). Tragically, Forbes's wife, children and servants were all killed. In this song, the horror of the incident does not preclude sympathetic portrayal of its all too human protagonists: here, we discover the motivation for Gordon's act (he longs to take 'that fair lady' while her lord is away, st 3); witness the lady's defiant remonstrances (st 10); her hurt at her servant's betrayal (st 12–14); and, most movingly of all, hear her children's frightened voices:

> O then bespake her youngest son,
>   Sat on the nurse's knee,
> 'Dear mother, gie owre your house,' he says,
>   'For the reek it worries me.' (st 15)

When her little girl falls only to be impaled upon Gordon's spear (st 18–19), the ballad here resembles a 'gothic' horror; but it is as interested in the psychological consequences of Gordon's act as disturbing us by its violence. Imagining how beautiful the girl might have grown to be, Gordon is filled with regret, and also dismay that 'brave Edom of Gordon / Was daunted with a dame' (st 23). Although the ballad ends in a fiery bloodbath (Forbes returns and kills Gordon's men in revenge and the last verse suggests that Gordon kills himself: 'At last into the flames he flew', st 29), it functions as an emotional, as much as a gothic, drama. In typical ballad style, the events and characters speak for themselves; no final comment or judgement is passed except that which we make ourselves in response to a story which is, at heart, about loss and bereavement.

(iv) 'Quiet' Voices of History: 'Marie Hamilton'

The ballad of 'Marie Hamilton' (Lyle 75) illustrates one of our initial premises that ballads may give voice to historically unrecorded experience, and shows how the ballad-maker's imagination can weave historical 'facts' into a 'new history' – a new imaginative whole. The song tells the story of one Marie Hamilton, here supposed to be one of the four 'Maries' who famously served Mary, Queen of Scots. By the third verse, we learn that Darnley, the Scottish king and Mary's second husband, is the father of the child whom she (Marie) has just murdered: 'Sink ye, swim ye, bonny wee babe! / You'l neer get mair o' me' (st 3). The baby's cries have been heard in the palace and the truth is discovered; her fate is to walk up the Canongate on the Royal Mile in Edinburgh to the Parliament where she is sentenced to execution for the crime of infanticide. Gradually, our initial horror at Marie's act is tempered by her growing humanity: from denying her guilt and choosing to wear a white dress so that she may 'shine through Edinbro town' (st 7), to being taunted and stumbling on 'the Parliament stair' (st 9). Marie knows full well there is no reprieve and, unexpectedly, drinks to 'the jolly sailors / That sail upon the sea / Let them never let on to my father and mother / That I cam here to dee' (st 14). Poignantly, she thinks of when her own mother 'cradled' her and her father 'held up me' (st 15, 16). Lyle notes that in fact none of the queen's four 'Maries' were accused of infanticide but that a Frenchwoman in the queen's service was hanged in 1563 for this crime and observes a similar incident involving one Mary Hamilton at the Russian court in 1719; both these historically verifiable women may have been the model for this ballad 'Mary'. Most importantly, the song brings to life from historical records one of a substantial number of young women who were tried and usually hung for infanticide in sixteenth-century Scotland. Without diminishing or denying the terrible nature of this crime, a historical ballad such as 'Marie Hamilton' portrays what may have been the most likely reality behind these criminal cases: a confused, naive and frightened young girl. A voice which would otherwise have been historically 'quiet' (silenced or suppressed) is made articulate, reinforcing our perception that the finest historical ballads tell stories of human drama. History is imaginatively woven into songs about lovers, heroes, nations, and ordinary people caught up in momentous events.

The Worlds of the Supernatural

In this section, the popular ballad world of the unnatural, the marvellous and the magical is explored; oral and folk traditions, traditional superstition and custom, and romance material inherited from Celtic storytellers shape its physical and psychological landscapes. Ballads deploy a variety of names for this world – a 'cuntrie' to which one is exiled, often without return, it may be called 'fairy land', 'elf land', 'hell' – but we shall simply use the all-encompassing term of the 'supernatural'. A panoply of diverse supernatural protagonists inhabit this particular corpus of songs: fairies, elfin knights, the Queen of Elfland and the 'King of the Fairies', witches, ghosts, seal-people, mermaids, and the Devil himself. Although an imaginative fascination with the 'otherworld' is found in most popular and traditional literatures (often a potent brew of classical, pagan and orthodox religious beliefs), it has frequently been categorised as a peculiarly distinctive feature of the Scottish ballad tradition. Its appeal, and hence pervasiveness, can be understood intuitively. Like all good ghost stories, the best supernatural ballads send proverbial shivers down our spine. Emotionally and psychologically powerful, they allow us to enter a world which expels the explicable and the rational, demanding that we believe, and trust, in the mysterious and the magical. Dreams and prophecies recur in such ballads, suggesting that fate or fortune, a destiny beyond human control, governs earthly life. Here, we shall explore recurrent supernatural types or 'characters' as well as the formal presentation, narrative functions and symbolic powers of the 'otherworldly'.

(i) Witches
As befits their depiction in traditional folklore and in popular superstition (in sixteenth-century Scotland supposed 'witches' were persecuted with particular enthusiasm by King James VI, helping to stoke the fires of popular cultural imagination), witches are rarely positive characters. The 'witch-woman' of 'The Broomfield Hill' (Lyle 40), for example, offers apparent help to a young woman who is unsure whether to meet her lover, a knight, at the eponymous hill and so lose her virginity, or stay at home and so risk being accused of unfaithfulness. The witch suggests she can do *both*, if she lays a sprig of broom next to him, and puts her rings on the fingers of his right hand. That way, he will know she has visited him but she will retain her purity. But when the

knight wakens in distress to find her gone, he blames his 'milk-white steed' and 'gay goss-hawk', who articulately defend themselves (speaking animals are common): 'I clapped wi my wings, master, / And aye my bells I rang, / And aye cry'd, Waken, waken, master, / Before the ladye gang' (st 12). The knight's instinctive love, and the loyalty and goodness of his animals, cannot defeat the witch's malign magic which has managed to destroy the young couple's love:

> 'Ye need na burst your gude white steed,
>   Wi racing oer the howm;
> Nae bird flies faster through the wood,
>   Than she fled through the broom.' (st 14)

(ii) Ghosts

The most popular spectral protagonist of the ballad world is 'the revenant': the spirit of a person who has died and returned to visit the earth, usually those to whom they were closest in life. The revenant inhabits the liminal space or threshold between the worlds of the living and the dead; symbolising the past but intruding on the present, they provoke a mixture of fear, love and longing in the mortals they leave behind.

(1) 'Son David'

In this ballad, a young man, David, appears before his mother, alarmingly bloodstained. She repeatedly asks 'what's the blood', unconvinced by his replies that it belongs first to his 'grey meer', then his 'greyhound', and next his 'huntin hawk', who would not obey him. Finally, we learn the awful truth: he has killed his brother, John, for exactly that reason – 'because he wadnae rule by me' (Lyle 66, st 8). David does not explain why or how but vows that he will disappear, forever, 'in a bottomless boat' (st 9). The stanza-by-stanza dialogue exchanges between mother and son are dramatically effective: strangely, but movingly, she seems to accept what has happened. Having asked only when he will 'come back again', David tells her, twice, 'when the sun an the moon meet in yon glen, / ... I'll return again' (st 11); in other words, as a ghost. That odd, astrological fusion of 'the sun and the moon' is a highly poetic expression which recurs in other supernatural ballads alluding to the time of the revenant's return. 'Son David' was sung by the famous ballad singer Jeannie Robertson, who suggested an explanation for David's murder of his brother: 'that David was the elder brother, that the younger brother was jealous

The Scottish Ballads

of his rights and possessions and attacked him, and that David's killing of his brother was an act of self-defence'.[16] The text itself betrays nothing of motive or purpose and, in so doing, aligns the audience's perspective with the mother's: like her, we simply witness David's final day on earth. The violence of the initial act is gradually annulled as our sympathies seem to turn to the mother who ultimately faces severance from not one but two sons.

(2) 'The Wife of Usher's Well'

The most well-known of 'revenant' ballads, 'The Wife of Usher's Well' (Lyle 31) also portrays the living, then ghostly, relationship between a mother and her three sons. First printed in Scott's *Minstrelsy*, 'from the recitation of an old woman residing near Kirkhill, in West Lothian', the ballad describes three 'stout and stalwart sons' who are sent to sea. By the third verse their mother learns that her drowned sons will never return. She prays that they will; and sure enough, maternal grief miraculously summons them back from the dead on a 'lang and mirk' night on Martinmas (St Martin's Day, 11 November). The ballad constructs a 'reality' composed of the ghostly and the mundane. While the mother prepares the house for their return (st 7–8), as though she were ordinarily welcoming them home, the brothers enter with hats made of a 'birk' (birch) which grows only 'at the gates of Paradise' (st 6). The birch symbolises their irrevocable separation from the living world and also the (comforting?) sign that they have reached heaven. Note how these Christian associations are evoked within the pagan context of the supernatural: 'Up then crew the red, red cock, / And up the crew the gray; / The eldest to the youngest said, / 'T is time we were away' (st 9). Along with these quasi-ritualistic manifestations of the supernatural, the ballad has tenderly human qualities (the sons not only bid farewell to their mother but to 'barn and byre', and 'the bonny lass / That kindles my mother's fire!' (st 12)). It is a ghost story but also a consolatory tale about death and loss. The mother has at least had a chance to see her sons one last time; the borders between the earthly and the supernatural have been breached, not to elicit fear, but temporarily to reunite, through the power of love, those whom death will separate for good.

(3) 'Sweet William's Ghost'

Peaceful reconciliation does not always stem from human communion with ghosts. In this 'revenant' ballad which appeared in Ramsay's *Tea-Table Miscellany*, a young woman called Margret is visited by her dead lover, Willy, 'from Scotland new come home' (Lyle 30, st 2). The ghost leaves Margret in no doubt that 'I am no earthly man' (st 6): '"it is but my spirit, Margret, / That's now speaking to thee"' (st 9). He wants her now to pledge the 'faith and troth' which he had promised her in life. Margret agrees, without realising that she must exchange her own life as well. She puts on 'her robes of green / A piece below her knee' (st 11), that formulaic act which symbolises female beauty and fertility, except that this time it takes place in 'the live-lang winter night' (st 11) and in a graveyard. Expecting to be reunited with her 'only true-love' (st 16), Margret instead sees him vanish at dawn, with a gothically 'grievous groan' (st 15). He turns out to be an unjustly punitive, rather than tender, ghost-lover for she immediately dies: 'Wan grew her cheeks, she closd her een / Stretchd her soft limbs, and dy'd' (st 16). The ballad ends on the fitting finality of the verb, 'dy'd', leaving us only to contemplate Margret's beautiful corpse, and the 'folly' of mortals who set out in pursuit of ghosts. This ballad epitomises what has been called the 'matter-of-fact' nature of the Scottish ballads' treatment of the supernatural.[17] The ghost's arrival 'at Margret's door' is dispassionately reported to the audience; and her fearless pursuit of his 'dead corp' (st 11) into the winter night is stated without elaboration. We simply assume, and do not question, that she loves him enough to lie with him in his coffin. This might indeed hold the key to the power of the revenant ballad genre: characters usually *want* to see the ghosts of their dead relations and lovers. Although the ballads purposefully conjure up ghostly manifestations which are (presumably) designed to elicit fear in their audience, they also depict a form of wish-fulfilment which has meaning from multiple perspectives, whether religious, superstitious or simply human: namely, that death is not the end.

(iii) The Devil and Malicious Enchantments

Manifestations of the demonic are also a popular characteristic of the supernatural Scottish ballad. In 'The Fause Knight' (Lyle 18), the Devil appears to a 'wee boy' on his way 'to the skeul', besieging him with questions until the boy finally manages to turn the curse upon the Devil. In 'The Daemon Lover' (Lyle 19), the titular 'hero' returns to his beloved after an absence of seven years (st 1), a time period which, in the ballad world, should alert us to the potential of its supernatural connotations. But his lover has married another man (st 2), which enrages him:

> He turned him right and round about,
>   And the tear blinded his ee:
> 'I wad never hae trodden on Irish ground,
>   If it had not been for thee.
>
> I might hae had a king's daughter,
>   Far, far beyond the sea;
> I might have had a king's daughter,
>   Had it not been for love o' thee.' (st 3–4)

The lady asks why she should now leave her husband and 'two babes'? He replies that he has eight ships, '"four-and-twenty bold mariners, / And music on every hand"' (st 7). With that, and the peculiar emotional logic of the ballad world, she steps onto the ship with her lover, without hesitation. Though it is a beautiful ship (the 'masts o' beaten gold' suggest an ethereal, fairy vessel), there are no sailors on board. Sure enough, the lover reveals his cloven hoof: he is the Devil himself, no less. At this point, the demon lover turns oddly lyrical, promising her sight of 'how the lilies grow / On the banks of Italy' (st 12). This promise is followed by another two: a vision of 'the hills of heaven' (st 13) and then, more darkly, a vision of 'the mountain of hell' (st 14). Hell is their final destination but not before, in the final stanza, the Devil has sunk their ship (st 15). The ballad is powerful, not least because of the sudden and stark revelation of the Devil's identity and the way in which, in characteristic ballad style, beauty abruptly turns to horror, love into fear.

The function of the supernatural is partly to bring about the unexpected and the quite impossible. Magic, often in the form of talismanic objects, charms, music, may work to metamorphose the ordinary into the unusual. One of the best, though most disturbing, examples of this metamorphosis motif which has devilish connotations, or at least associations of black magic, is the ballad of 'The Twa Magicians' (Lyle 39). The two protagonists are a lady, who 'stands in her bower door, / As straight as willow wand' and a blacksmith poised 'wi hammer in his hand' (st 1). These descriptions simultaneously convey an image of female uprightness (symbolic purity) and masculine aggression; appropriately so, for the 'coal-black smith' wants the lady's 'maidenhead' (st 2) – or virginity. She swears she would rather die; he, however, is adamant ('I'll cause ye be …'). The pattern of his coercion, and her resistance, assumes magical, metamorphic form for the next eight verses as she assumes one animal form, thinking to elude him, and he another. The magical forms which they incarnate take an increasingly bizarre turn: 'a het girdle and a cake', a 'ship and nail', a 'silken plaid and green covering'. But through this shape-shifting, the blacksmith attains union with her:

> Then she became a gay grey mare,
>   And stood in yonder slack,
> And he became a gilt saddle,
>   And sat upon her back. (st 11)

Here, metamorphosis is not a form of liberation but ultimately one of entrapment for the young woman. For contemporary audiences, this becomes a dark, sinister tale of sexual violation. The alignment of sexual violence with the motif of metamorphosis evokes classical myth, particularly the Greek myth, retold by the Latin poet Ovid, of Philomela, raped by Tereus, King of Thrace, and changed into a bird.

(iv) Ballad 'Morality' and the Psychology of the Supernatural

Ballads such as 'The Twa Magicians', 'The Daemon Lover' and others raise interesting questions about the ethical scope and nature of the ballads: do they have a moral 'message'? Are they intended to teach or instruct, as well as entertain? Critics have questioned whether the supernatural ballads, with their range of pagan and folkloric symbolism and superstition, can be understood within the orthodox Christian moral framework which undoubtedly defined the pre-twentieth-century communities from which the songs emerge. Yet, for example, it could be argued that 'The Daemon Lover', in charting symbolic paths to heaven and hell, portrays its tempted female character as an Eve-like figure no less.

Though moral interpretations can be proposed, it is striking how much attention, in terms of narrative portrayal and psychological interest, the ballads actually devote to the depiction of 'moral transgression'. Put simply, ballads (especially the supernatural type) explore the 'darker' aspects of the human psyche. This assertion holds true about other forms of traditional and popular literature. What Maria Tatar says about the violence and emotion of some fairy stories could equally well be said of the ballads: 'Fairy tales take us into a world where taboos may still be in force but where transgression is the motor of the plot'.[18] In

1975, the German psychoanalyst Bruno Bettelheim (1903–90) famously argued in *The Uses of Enchantment* that fairy stories 'externalise' (or translate into concrete events, characters, images) internal psychological processes. Fundamental human emotions, such as fear, anxiety, and the need for love, are mirrored in their universal, or 'archetypal', story patterns. For children, they can perform a positive emotional role; since most fairy tales have happy endings, they show how fear and loneliness, for example, can be overcome.

The 'enchantment' at work in the supernatural ballads differs, of course; but, like fairy stories, ballads can communicate both 'overt and covert' meanings – the significance of events, and the language in which they are conveyed, may be obvious ('overt') or hidden ('covert', concealed by symbol and metaphor). In this 'double' way, their peculiar stories and symbols carry psychological power: they are ways of exploring, and 'externalising', complex emotions such as desire and love. Deep or profound feelings can thus be 'safely' mediated by, or enclosed within, stories of fantasy. In 'Sweet William's Ghost', Margret's supernatural lover might be understood as a symbolic projection of her *own* erotic or sexual desire; the unknown, and fearful, territory into which it might lead her.

Ultimately, supernatural ballads possess the power to tell us about *our selves* – all of our known and hidden depths (our conscious and unconscious realms) – just as they enchant, and sometimes horrify, us. Perhaps our tendency to 'rationalise' or look for moral purpose in 'The Daemon Lover' and other songs defeats the purpose, analogous to how modern editors often 'edit out' the dark undertones of violence and eroticism in the nineteenth-century fairy stories of the Grimm brothers. Indeed, Willa Muir wryly notes how Walter Scott dealt with the ambiguous erotic power of 'Tam Lin' (explored below): 'He's taen her by the milk-white hand / Among the leaves sae green / And what they did I cannot tell / The green leaves were between'.[19]

(v) Two 'Eerie' Fairy Tales

The enduringly popular and well-loved ballads of 'Tam Lin' and 'Thomas the Rhymer' are thematically linked in their stories of a mortal (in both instances, a young man) who is abducted by fairies. The motif of fairy abduction has long-established roots in medieval folktale and legend; for example, one of the twelfth-century *lais* of Marie de France depicts how the Arthurian knight Sir Lanval is spirited away to the Isle of Avalon by the beautiful *fey* or fairy for whom he renounces everything. The legendary fate of Thomas the Rhymer, the thirteenth-century poet known as Thomas of Erceldoune (or Earlston), echoes Lanval's in its retellings in romance and ballad traditions; while Tam Lin's seizure by the Queen of Elfland is only temporary, thanks to the heroic efforts of the girl on earth who loves him. Both ballads are fine illustrations of the supernatural ballad tradition's rich weave of symbol and emotion.

(1) 'Tam Lin' (Lyle 35): human love versus Elfland's power

Stanzas 1–7 The ballad's first verse is a warning: 'O I forbid you, maidens a', / That wear gowd on your hair, / To come or gae by Carterhaugh, / For young Tam Lin is there.' This warning, issuing from an unidentified narrative voice, implies that Tam Lin threatens the purity, or virginity, of beautiful young women. At once Janet, our heroine, disobeys this injunction (the first of her many disavowals of 'authority') by 'kilt[ing] her green kirtle', braiding her hair, and journeying to the forbidden place. When she plucks a rose, 'up ... started young Tam Lin' who enquires '...why breaks thou the wand ... / why comes thou to Carterhaugh / Withoutten my command?' (st 6). Janet has arrived unsolicited by Tam and, though she does not reveal why she uprooted the rose, an audience, attuned to the conventions of ballad symbolism, might metaphorically interpret Janet's act as willing the loss of virginity (the rose is a conventional emblem of feminine purity). In defying Tam, she also seems boldly to lay claim to Carterhaugh.

Stanzas 8–16 Verse 8 in this version, a narrative interlude in which Janet returns home, is stanzaically different from the other four-line verses. At her father's castle, 'four and twenty' gentlewomen (a formulaic phrase) are playing courtly games, suggesting the ballad's medieval setting. Janet, however, is the most beautiful: 'as green as onie glass', a lovely, if rather strange, phrase, again associates her beauty with the symbol green and its connotations of spring and fertility. When rebuked by an elderly knight, as well as her father, she defends herself. If she is indeed pregnant, as they suspect, it is her own responsibility. Unlike other ballad young women, stolen or preyed upon by men, she has, *of her own volition,* found her 'true-love'. We, the audience, now realise that in the apparent narrative gap between verses 7 and 8 Janet and Tam have made love. The description of her beloved's silver- and gold-shod horse in stanza 16 begins to alert us that he may not be 'an earthly knight'.

Stanzas 17–21 Verse 17 is another six-line verse transition in which Janet returns to Carterhaugh. In order to summon Tam, she repeats her earlier action but this time, Tam is alarmed: is she trying 'to kill the bonie babe / That we gat us between'? (st 20). Now we know that they are lovers; but it is left unexplained (narrative ellipsis is a common ballad feature, leaving our own imagination to fill the gaps) why Janet's gesture might endanger the child's life. Instead, she is concerned that her beloved may be unbaptised: '"If eer ye was in holy chapel, or christendom did see?"' (st 21). In other words, she too suspects he is not mortal. The conventional nature of Janet's piety also highlights the disparity between the 'ordinariness' of her world and the unearthly adventure she will shortly experience after Tam has told her the strange fairy tale of his life.

Stanzas 22–35 Tam confesses what has happened: abducted by the Queen of the Fairies, he was taken to 'yon green hill to dwell' (st 23); it was popularly believed that the fairy folk (in Gaelic, the *Sluagh Sidhe* or the People of Peace) lived beneath the hills, especially so in Highland fairy superstition. Fairy land is 'pleasant' enough, he tells Janet, but warns that 'at the end of seven years / We pay a tiend to hell; / I am sae fair and fu o' flesh, / I'm feard it be mysel' (st 24). The idea of a dark, literally hellish, fairy world is at first startling, contrary to our popular notions of benign fairies inherited from Victorian conceptions. In fact, traditional Scottish fairy belief conceived of fairy land as the country of the dead, and of the fairies themselves as fallen angels. The frequently malign mischief-making of 'fairy-related creatures', bogles and brownies in folktale and legend is thus explicable within this belief system. Tam's only means of escape is that very night, Halloween, when the boundaries between the worldly and the unworldly realms may transiently be breached, and specifically at midnight, the hour of the 'fairy ride'. Only then can mortals attempt to win back their stolen 'true love'. Tam tells her exactly what will happen: how he will look, what horse he shall ride, and all the alarming metamorphoses he will go through before he will be transformed into a 'naked knight'.

Stanzas 36–42 Courageously, Janet has undertakes to rescue her beloved. On a 'gloomy' Hallows Eve, she finds her way to Miles Cross. Sure enough, events unfold just as Tam has predicted. Descriptive detail is delicately used. When Janet hears the fairy bridles ring, she is 'as glad at that / As any earthly thing' (st 37), which is, of course, ironic since it is a decidedly *un*earthly sound. It is no mean feat to steal the 'boniest knight' from the 'angry' Fairy

Queen, who resembles the wicked queens of fairy tales rather than Shakespeare's Titania; she bitterly curses Janet: 'Shame betide her ill-far'd face, / And an ill death may she die' (st 41). Such characterisation firmly aligns our sympathies with the song's human protagonists. The Fairy Queen declares that had she known Tam would elude her she 'wad hae taen out thy twa grey een / And put in twa een o' tree' (st 42); in other words, blinded him so that he would never have contemplated Janet's beauty.

Unusually, 'Tam Lin' is a ballad which depicts the mortal or human world triumphing over the otherworldly. Janet's buoyant human energy and resilience conquers the resentful powers of the fairies; we, the audience, share joy and relief with our eponymous hero and his rescuer. Janet is a popular ballad heroine because she reverses the 'natural' relationship in traditional romance between the knight and his lady; in 'Tam Lin', the supposedly heroic 'earthly knight' (st 29) who betrays vulnerability and not the young woman who undertakes the trials of the romance hero. The strength of her love, both for Tam, her 'bairn's father' (st 31), and her child, makes Janet hold fast to her alarmingly metamorphosing knight. This truly life-affirming ballad celebrates the miraculous power of tenacious love. Even though this version ends with the Fairy Queen's curse, and the destructive emotions of jealousy and hatred, we sense that neither has any force; the positive energies of Janet, 'as blythe's a bird in spring', are much too great. The ballad presents two examples of the power of female love: one destructive in its intensity, the other creative and regenerative. Metamorphosis is perhaps the ballad's key theme: the fantastic shape-changing of Tam's 'rebirth' into the earthly realm symbolises the transformative power of love itself.

(2) 'Thomas the Rhymer' (Lyle 36): 'Elfland' and the realm of the spiritual

Stanza 1 Typically of ballad narration, we begin in the middle of the action: Thomas, lying on a riverbank in the Eildon Hills in the Borders, glimpses a 'lady bright' approaching on horseback. His name, 'True Thomas', identifies him with the historical character Thomas of Ercildoune (1219–99), who lived in the reign of Alexander III. The epithet 'true' derives from his alleged capture by the Queen of Fairyland when he was given the power of prophecy (he could only speak the truth). This legend is also portrayed in the popular medieval romance, *Thomas of Ercildoune*. From the outset, then, the audience associates Thomas with the powers of poetry, eloquence and 'truth'.

Stanza 2 At this moment, Thomas does not know the identity of the beautiful maiden but her 'otherworldliness' is suggested by her dress of 'grass-green silk' and the impossibly lovely 'fifty siller bells and nine' which hang from her horse's mane.

Stanza 3 Thomas thinks that this unearthly beauty might be the Virgin Mary herself, and genuflects before her. This is one of the most interesting religious references in the ballad corpus, which is often characterised as pagan or largely irreligious. This miraculous Marian vision conveys Thomas's intuitive piety, and roots the ballad and its origins in a medieval and Catholic spiritual framework. Though this proves to be a fairy, rather than angelic, queen, it suggests that this ballad is infused with a distinctive 'spirituality'.

Stanzas 4–8 Revealing herself as 'the queen of fair Elfland', she has deliberately sought out Thomas. Using the chant, 'Harp and carp along wi me', she challenges Thomas to a distinctly 'unspiritual' exchange: 'if ye dare to kiss my lips, / Sure of your bodie I will be' (st 5). Careless of what might happen (the term 'weird' introduces the concept of fate or destiny), Thomas does indeed kiss her, 'on the rosy lips', under the Eildon Tree. His fate is sealed: he is bound to serve the Fairy Queen for seven years (the repetition of 'maun' (must) stresses the inevitability of this unholy alliance).

Stanzas 8–10 Thomas is abducted. This is portrayed both visually and aurally – the bells of the fairy horse ring out as it speeds 'swifter than the wind' – and by the effective device of repetition (the verb phrases give all narrative agency to the powerful queen). Their unnatural journey culminates in arrival at 'a desert wide', pointedly beyond 'living land'. The desert suggests it could be a wilderness (which has biblical connotations), or a remote, quasi-exotic landscape.

Stanzas 10–14 Tenderly, the Fairy Queen lays Thomas's head on her knee but then conjures up 'ferlies three': visions of three roads, one narrow, one 'braid' and one 'bonny'. They must take only one. Here, the ballad seems to reflect the style and conventions of medieval allegory (the Greek-derived word 'allegory' literally means 'to speak otherwise'): this is a symbolic landscape. In fact, the Queen provides her own explanations. The first, 'the path of righteousness', clearly symbolises the arduous path to heaven; the imagery of 'thorns and briers', evoking Christ's crown of thorns, suggesting that one walks this as a pilgrim. The second is the road to hell; its 'wickedness' is tempting to follow, as the Queen ironically suggests it's often mistaken for 'the road to heaven'. But it's the third road which Thomas and the Queen will take, as anyone alert to ballad numerology would have guessed: 'the road to fair Elfland' (st 13) is notably 'bonny' and circuitous. Before they depart, the queen warns that Thomas must be sworn to secrecy, or else he will never return to his 'awin countrie' (a common phrase in the ballads, embodying ideas of journeying, return and exile from the familiar and loved).

Stanzas 15–17 The next three stanzas vividly portray their journey to 'Elfyn land'. The formulaic phrase, 'O they rade on, and farther on', its rhythmic stresses enacting ceaseless onward movement, precedes an account of a journey defined by its curious removal from ordinary diurnal time ('they saw neither sun nor moon'), and felt keenly through sound and sensation: 'the roaring of the sea' and the tidal motions of rivers. Entrenched in black night, they 'waded through red blude to the knee'. What does this horrifying image mean? If it refers to 'a' the blude that's shed on earth', is it to be interpreted in a Christian sense? Is 'that countrie' (fairy land?) a kind of Purgatory (a place of temporary suffering where dying souls expiate, or make amends for, their sins)? Finally, they enter 'a garden green'. Given the ballad's intertwining of pagan and biblical language, this evokes the Garden of Eden. The Fairy Queen, like another Eve, pulls an apple (the biblical fruit of the tree of knowledge): 'Take this for thy wages, True Thomas, / It will give thee the tongue that can never lie' (st 17). Coming from the Queen of Elfland, this seems a suspect gift: is it a blessing or a curse?

Stanzas 18–19 For sure, Thomas would rather the Queen keep her 'gudely gift': he'd rather dispose of it 'at fair or tryst where I may be'! With sudden humility, Thomas vows he wouldn't dare speak to anyone, 'prince or peer', or 'fair layde'. But the Queen only imposes an injunction of silence by virtue of her own authority. The ballad ends suddenly, as if to mirror the unquestionable logic of the Queen's own enigmatic but absolute statement: 'For as I say, so it must be'. The final stanza epitomises the stark brevity of ballad endings: all we are left with is the knowledge that poor Thomas, for the next seven years, wore 'a coat of the even cloth' and shoes 'of velvet green', and was not seen on earth all that time.

'Thomas the Rhymer' exemplifies many key features of the supernatural ballad: the way in which the human and the otherworld suddenly meet across a magical threshold; the vulnerability of mortals before fairy or supernatural agency; the power of imagery as a descriptive and symbolic tool so that it, as much as the strange or uncanny events of the ballad, carries meaning; and the force of erotic desire to set events in motion. The ballad intensifies these aspects so that we have a tale that draws us in closely to its enigmatic heart and yet ultimately resists our 'common sense' attempts to decipher its meaning. It brings two rich symbolic discourses together: the folkloristic and pagan, with the Christian, specifically Roman Catholic. These open up the song's imaginative horizons, with its allusions to heaven, hell, blood, tree and apple, and implies that it embraces complex religious or spiritual ideas. Is this song about the nature of sin (does Thomas 'fall', or is he punished, because he is tempted? And by what: the beauty of the Fairy Queen, or the desire to disobey?), or about the curse of 'knowledge' (so that the ballad enacts, allegorically speaking, original sin)? The ballad portrays a world which is certainly fearful but also beautiful. If one wanted to take a moralistic view of the ballad, it could be read as a warning against the duplicity of beauty: the way in which our senses, and sexual desire, can deceive us. And since Thomas was reputed to be a poet, is the ballad about poetic power itself: its ability to conjure up strange and fabled worlds? Such is its richness that it is open to interpretations, whether psychological, religious, or moral. And it's a very fine story too.

(vi) Selkies and Mermaids: Fables of Love and Ecology

Although the famous 'selkie' (meaning 'seal' in Orkney dialect) ballads are included in this section, we recognise that these marvellous creatures, half-human, half-animal, belong to the mythic imagination, rather than the 'supernatural' proper. The selkie legends emerge from a wealth of traditional folklore surrounding water and its variety of spirits (such as water demons, kelpies, the water-bull and water-horse of the Highlands); in Celtic tradition, they are sometimes believed to be a kind of fairy, or children of the King of Lochlann. It is easy to understand why seals, frequently seen in Scottish coastal waters, with their gentle faces and curious eyes, have been endowed with human qualities. The selkie legends in particular demonstrate how storytelling arises from long-held desires simultaneously to explain and mystify the natural world. Both selkie men and women were reputed to be beautiful; traditional tales and folklore often focus on erotic encounters between them and mortals.[20] The well-known ballad discussed below, which exists in many versions, is from Orkney (the words and tune first collected on the island of Flotta in 1938).

'The Great Silkie of Sule Skerry' (Lyle 34)

Stanza 1 The ballad begins gently: 'an eartly nourris' (earthly nurse) sings a lullaby to her child; the foregrounded word, 'earthly', makes us think of its opposite, the 'unearthly'. Her song is sad; she knows nothing of the 'bairnis father', not least, and most mysteriously, 'the land that he staps in'.

Stanza 2 As if magically summoned by this lament, a 'grumly guest' (so described by our narrator, witnessing events) appears, revealing himself as the child's father.

Stanza 3 We learn his identity by means of rhythmic, incantatory language: 'I am a man, upo the lan' / An I am a silkie in the sea / And when I'm far and far frae lan, / My dwelling is in Sule Skerrie'. The devices of internal rhyme, assonance and alliteration sensually portray his shape-shifting. Selkies assume human form when they shed their sealskin; the skin holds the power of magical transformation.

Stanza 4 Echoing language, not only of 'Sule Skerrie' but the woman's lament, 'It was na weel', immediately provokes our sympathy and concern, presaging danger, though we have been intrigued by the selkie himself who is clearly known by reputation.

Stanza 5 Suddenly, it seems as though their union is entirely loveless since the selkie demands his son from the boy's mother ('Gie to me ... / tak thee up'), and gives her 'a purse of goud', her 'nourris-fee', as though the young woman has only cared for him temporarily. Her voice is not heard again.

Stanza 6 The selkie begins to prophesy; note the way in which the conjunctive 'an' (and) is used repeatedly to link each verse line, lending his prediction an inevitability. The first prophecy is tender and beautiful; the selkie-child will learn to 'swim the faem' on a hot 'simmer's day'.

Stanza 7 The second prophecy is a complete reversal of the idyllic communion foreshadowed between father and child: he predicts the girl, the baby's mother, will go on to marry 'a proud gunner' who will kill both the selkie-man and child. It is a shocking ending as the selkie imagines a brutal death. Our emotional sympathies have changed: where we pitied the girl, seemingly used as a vessel to create the selkie-child, now we see the bonds of love in the selkies' world threatened by human cruelty. There is no such thing as a clear moral universe in the ballads. Like other selkie ballads, this song also serves as a timeless ecological, or environmental, fable; nature's creatures should be left well alone.

*

Human communion with the seal people rarely ends happily. In the ballad 'Clark Colven' (Lyle 33), where the dangerous liaison is between a young man and a 'mermaiden', the outcome is nothing less than death. For original audiences, mermaids were rarely the gentle creatures of the famous Hans Christian Andersen story but, according to folklore and legend, characterised more by their dangerous beauty. Orkney and Shetland are the source of many mermaid, or 'merfolk', tales. In this ballad, as in 'Tam Lin', a warning is defied: a knight's lady warns him of the lovely maiden who lives by 'the wall o' Stream'. At first it seems he'll be immune to the latter's charms ('"For I nae saw a fair woman / I like so well as thee"', st 3) but when he sees her bathing, with her 'milk-white' beauty, he forgets his beloved. Having slept with the 'mermaiden', he is afflicted by a headache which nothing will cure. In response, the mermaid merely laughs ('"It will ay be war till ye be dead"', st 10). When he tries to kill her, she metamorphoses into a fish and escapes; the knight returns home to die. The quiet, emotional expressiveness of the ballad style informs the penultimate verse: '"Oh, mither, mither, mak my bed, / And, gentle ladie, lay me down: / Oh, brither, brither, unbend my bow, / 'T will never be bent by me again." ' (st 13). The simple, almost ritualistic acts which he asks those whom he loves to carry out for him (which they do, mirrored in the imitative patterning of the final stanza) implies they do not punish him. As the maiden returns to her beautiful but deathly mermaid form, so the ballad ends poignantly.

(vii) Postscript: when the Supernatural isn't the Supernatural

The supernatural ballads blur the boundaries between the known and the unknown, the explicable and the mysterious – so much so that ballad characters themselves often find it difficult to decipher their world. What can *seem* to be the work of the otherworld sometimes proves not to be, as in the ballad 'Love Gregor' (Lyle 58). Here, a young girl, Fair Annie, so longs to see her beloved, who 'could no come hame', that she crosses the 'sa't sea fame' with her little son. When she arrives at her 'love's castle', Gregor's mother answers her anxious knocking but refuses to let her in, supposedly believing her a supernatural creature: 'Awa, awa ye ill woman / You'r nae come here for good / You'r but some witch, or wile warlock / or mer-maid of the flood' (st 10). When Gregor furiously realises what has happened, he rushes down to the shore but it is too late; Annie has set sail again, this time into a storm, and is drowned. No strange or uncanny force brings tragedy but the uncharitableness, indeed positive malevolence, of the mother-figure. Her unwillingness to believe in the 'truth' of Annie's love is the most 'unnatural' thing here. Just as this ballad sets up the possibility of supernatural meaning only to debunk it, so sometimes what is most to be feared in the ballad world is simply emotional cruelty, and not supernatural enchantment.

Ballad Women: Female Singers, Characters and Stories

The writer Robert Graves once claimed that ballads are 'no-one's property' so it may seem unfair to suggest that there is a particularly deep and long-held association between women and ballad creation. Yet it has been pointed out, 'women's names have long been associated with traditional Scottish balladry and song – as possible authors, certainly as tradition-bearers ...'[21] Men, of course, were and continue to be ballad tradition-bearers too; but it remains striking how many of the well-known ballad singers were women. One reason for this is that the social, domestic and labour patterns of women within traditional communities nurtured this particular kind of creativity. In northern Italy, for example, in the 1800s, women ballad singers came from large, rural families where the collective experience of work allowed them to sing and compose together; a way to pass or endure the time but also to preserve cultural traditions. Popular song, storytelling and women's work are similarly connected in Highland culture. In this section, we shall briefly consider several important female ballad singers from a variety of backgrounds before exploring how the representation of women in the songs may serve to reflect and dramatise specifically female concerns.

(i) Voices and Singers

The eighteenth-century singer Anna Gordon, usually known by her married name, Anna Brown of Falkland (she is popularly called 'Mrs Brown of Falkland'), has one of the most extensive ballad repertoires (fifty-one versions of thirty-eight ballads are attributed to her). In the nineteenth century we find a number of singers, such as Agnes Lyle, who lived in Kilbarchan, and Mary Macqueen Storie and Meg Walker Caldwell, both from the village of Lochwinnoch. These are only the women whose songs were transcribed by antiquarian collectors in this period; the voices, and songs, of women whom such men as William Motherwell, William Tytler and Robert Chambers did *not* meet or know, go unrecorded. The manuscripts of Anna Gordon's ballads, commissioned by Tytler, were used by Walter Scott for his *Minstrelsy*; the songs of Macqueen and Walker were preserved by Andrew Crawfurd, who lovingly devoted several years to gathering the traditional ballads and songs of his village, Lochwinnoch. Women's traditional song culture was therefore a crucial part of this widespread, determined effort to preserve

Scottish balladry; one song collector urged: 'May I entreat the aid of gentlewomen in Scotland, or elsewhere, who remember ballads that they have heard repeated by their grandmothers or nurses?'[22] Memory and oral transmission are the means by which these women learnt their ballads: Anna Brown inherited her songs from her aunt, her mother and a maidservant. Although these women are aligned in how they transmit the ballad tradition, the social and cultural environments in which they grew up differ profoundly. Anna Brown was the daughter of a professor of Classics at Aberdeen University and married the minister of Falkland. Agnes Lyle, on the other hand, was the daughter of a Paisley weaver whose life, in this poor, industrial region, would have been worlds apart from the genteel affluence of Anna Brown's. Traditional balladry, however, provides a bridge between such varying lives. The travelling community also links renowned female ballad singers of the late eighteenth and nineteenth centuries, such as Mary Macqueen, with the great twentieth century singers, such as Jeannie Robertson, a 'settled urbanised "traveller" (or tinker)', who learnt many ballads from her aunt, Maggie, and who is rooted in this important Scottish tradition of female ballad singers.

It has been suggested that the songs such women as Agnes Lyle chose to perpetuate were a kind of 'conduit' through which social and political concerns, such as issues of class and gender, could be channelled. The seemingly archetypal situations which afflict ballad protagonists, such as loss, abandonment, or betrayal between lovers of different social status, acquire specific resonance, not only for Agnes but for the community for whom she sings. Accordingly, ballads come to possess not only an emotionally cathartic power but a social and political function too; a singer and her audience can explore the material as well as the emotional conditions of life. The repertoire of female ballad singers, however, is usually characterised as stereotypically 'feminine', favouring songs which deal with love, marriage and childbirth. This might seem a narrow view of female creativity and interests. But if we recall that the popularity and longevity of the ballad form is partly because it makes meaningful, by way of symbolic or archetypal stories, aspects of the human condition, then it should not surprise us that women should narrate their own specific life experiences and stories. For many traditional, non-literate, communities, it was important, and natural, that a female singer should dramatise these for a female audience.

(ii) Maidens, Temptresses, Heroines and Jealous Sisters

Most ballads originate in a culture which could not offer women social and political equality; that they should typically portray women within the context of marriage and family should not surprise us. Yet the range of central or archetypal female roles and 'predicaments' in the ballads are more varied and interesting than is often assumed. I shall suggest that there are five archetypal ballad women: the innocent maiden, the desiring lover, the romance heroine, the female wit, the bad woman (the last is the broadest category, encompassing negative female characters from jealous sisters and fairy-tale wicked stepmothers to murderous lovers).

(1) The Innocent Maiden

The first example of this character type is the young woman, usually beautiful and good, who is tragically sacrificed for love: think of Margret in 'Sweet William's Ghost' (Lyle 30), or Sara who dies 'for the lad I lost in Yarrow' ('The Dowie Dens o' Yarrow', Lyle 60, st 14). Broadly, this figure represents purity and innocence. A vast quantity of folksong dramatises what one ballad calls 'the last o' a' her maiden days' ('The Earl of Rosslyn's Daughter', Lyle 16, st 18); that is, a young girl's loss of virginity and/or her marriage. One unusual variant of the 'virginity' ballad is 'The Maid of Coldingham' (Lyle 32). A young 'may' (girl) is washing at a well when an 'eldren man' asks to drink its water. She refuses and suddenly her song, 'I am the fair maid of Coldingham', is used against her by the vengeful man who accuses her of having had 'seven bairns' (and of murdering six!). We never discover the truth of his accusation; but the dark, malevolent point of the ballad is to suggest that a beautiful, pure 'maid' may not be all that she seems. While this song portrays the young woman as an ambivalent figure, in the ballad world as a whole female purity has important and generally positive symbolic power.

Other 'virginity'-themed ballads are rooted in a distinctly realised social world where a girl's marriage destiny has real material and emotional consequences. In 'Gil Brenton' (Lyle 41), sung by Anna Brown, the bride has all the material comforts that she desires but still weeps. She misses her mother (st 14) and finds herself in a 'strange country'. Although this song has folkloric and romance qualities, it epitomises one of the most important female ballad experiences: marriage as an (initially) anxious, lonely or bewildering transition. In 'Donald of the Isles' (Lyle 12), this is given a more complex, delicate twist. Lizzie, an Edinburgh girl, is courted by a Highland lad: '"Will ye gang to the Hielands, Lizzie

Lindsay? / Will ye gae to the Hielands wi me?"' (st 4) "'How can I gang wi thee? / I dinna ken where I am gaing, / Nor wha I am gaing wi.'" (st 6). Her question to Nelly, her maid, touchingly evokes her vulnerability: "'Wad ye leave your father and mither, / And awa wi that fellow wad gae?'" (st 11). Lizzie's sense of exile and estrangement (even shown linguistically since she can't understand their Gaelic (st 19)) captures the predicament of the young woman on the threshold of sexual maturity and social convention. Lizzie's fate has a fairy-tale ending: Donald turns out to be an aristocratic lord so we might argue that such ballads symbolise not only a dream of romantic love but one of social aspiration and material wealth too. Personal or emotional fulfilment is often imagined in terms of social elevation in the symbolic language of ballads and fairy tales; entering the aristocracy 'represents' conjugal or marital happiness. Interestingly when Donald asks, 'Do you see yon bonnie braw castle? / Lady o' it ye will be' (st 23), we do not hear Lizzie's answer; her fulfilment is only imagined.

(2) Desiring Women
The antithesis of the gentle, self-sacrificing virgin is the woman who freely and boldly expresses her desires. Typically, the desiring ballad woman is 'otherworldly', a beautiful, if not dangerous, fairy mistress, but there are exceptions. In the ballad 'Johny Faa, the Gypsy Laddie' (Lyle 13), an aristocratic lady leaves her lord for a gypsy boy: "'I'll go to bed to my Johny Faa, / I'll go to bed to my deary …'" (st 6). When her lord discovers the truth, her serving men are 'a' put down' (st 10). Adulterous female desire not only results in a violation of marriage but is combined with an act of 'social' transgression. As Lyle notes, 'the mention of "the glamer" … suggests that she did not have control over her actions, but other verses imply that she was very willing'.[23]

The expression of female desire is not always portrayed as straightforwardly transgressive. In 'The Wind Hath Blown my Plaid Away' (Lyle 15; the refrain is sung by an elfin knight), a young girl's erotic longings magically summon a knight to her bed: "'I wish that horn were in my kist, / Yea, and the knight in my armes two'" (st 3). However, the excessive demands they make of each other eventually reveal that he has 'seven bairns' and a wife and so she decides to retain her 'maidenhead' (st 19). The young girl of 'The Place Where My Love Johnny Dwells' (Lyle 21) shows that persistence pays off. About to set off on an unexplained journey from which he may not return, Johnny insists that she should 'gang nae farther wi him' (st 5); she asserts that she 'wouldna bide' (st 4).

The Scottish Ballads　　　　　　　　　　　　　　　　　　49

This continues at every town they pass through until he buys her a wedding ring, confessing that she has 'stown [stolen] this heart o' mine' (st 9). While it might appear that poor Johnny simply gives in, the song might also be seen as a celebration of strong, intuitive female desire; love flourishes if one believes in its essential goodness. While 'Tam Lin' is the best illustration of that theme, other ballads portray bold, articulate young women who assert their love: 'The Shepherd's Dochter' (Lyle 43) is a particularly interesting example in which an eloquent shepherdess goes to the king's court to seek the prince who 'has taen my maidenhead / The flower of my bodye' (st 14) and whom she now considers is hers, regardless of conventional social or moral proprieties.

Desiring women in the ballad world, then, can upset the established moral and social order but the dispassionate, non-judgemental tone of the ballads refuses either to condemn or celebrate their 'waywardness'; in that sense, perhaps, these 'heroines' are liberated from conventional opinion.

(3) The Romance Heroine

The quality of persistence which characterised the heroine of 'The Place Where My Love Johnny Dwells' becomes heroic determination in the romance heroine type. 'Young Bicham' (Lyle 22), sung by Anna Brown of Falkland, reverses the conventional deliverance pattern of romance by having the heroine, 'Shusy Pye', liberate the young Englishman being held captive by her father. Not only that but when seven years have passed, and he hasn't returned to her 'strange' (apparently Middle Eastern) country to marry her, she embarks on a quest to find him. The ballad inherits the medieval romance's belief in fatalism (their love 'fated' to endure), and its disregard for the conventions of time and space: her journey is almost magically achieved. Unfortunately, when she arrives at 'Young Bicham's gates' (st 12), he is about to be married. But in this romance world, intuition and instinctive love prevail: Bicham chooses her as his bride instead, and she is rechristened 'Lady Jane'. In this female character, healing and restorative powers are combined with independence and courage (though where we might interpret her conversion from Islam to Christianity as a renunciation of her own true identity, it reflects the conventional, religious world view of medieval European romance). Other romance heroines include Janet in 'Tam Lin'; and the women who bravely defend and deliver their men from danger in 'Bog o' Gight' (Lyle 52) and 'The Laird o' Logie' (Lyle 53).

(4) The Female Wit

This character type relies on her wits and ingenuity to escape from tricky or dangerous situations. In 'The Gowans Sae Gay' (Lyle 14), Isabel outwits the elf-knight, indeed disposing of him in revenge for the seven young women he killed; in the ballad world, violence may justify violence, and women, surprisingly, can administer it. In 'The Gay Goss Hawk' (Lyle 57), an English girl, forbidden to marry her Scottish lover by her family, persuades her father that if she dies, she must be buried in Scotland. She is a happy version of Shakespeare's Juliet: having taken a 'sleepy draught' (st 19) to feign death, she is duly taken to be laid in northern soil only to revive and tell her seven brothers to 'boast in southin lans / Your sister's playd you scorn' (st 28).

(5) The Bad Woman

The ballad world offers up many versions of the equivalent fairy tale type of the wicked witch. Apart from supernaturally malevolent figures, ballad women who are 'negative' characters range from the fairly mild, almost entirely folkloric, shrew, who so harangues her husband that she's taken away by the Devil ('The Farmer's Curst Wife', Lyle 51), to the archetype of the resentful or cruel mother (e.g. 'The Drowned Lovers', Lyle 59) and, ultimately, to the woman capable of violent murder (see the 'Lady Macbeth' type characters of 'Earl Richard' (Lyle 76), 'Lord Ronald' (Lyle 78) and 'Lamkin' (Lyle 72). The most interesting ballads are those which portray the emotional and psychological reasons for women who act violently and in hatred. The ballad of 'Lord Thomas and Fair Annet' (Lyle 28) depicts the tragic consequences of rivalry between women. Thomas must choose to marry either the 'nut-brown' bride who has wealth or Annet, who has beauty but which, according to his mother, unlike wealth, will fade. Immediately, we recognise the archetypal, fairy-tale pattern of female beauty (fairness versus darkness, morally meaningful as well as physical). Thomas listens to his family's counsel and chooses the nut-brown maid. Urged by her father, Annet goes to the church to 'see that rich weddeen' (st 13): riding to the church she is so lovely that she would be mistaken for a bride, the 'siller bells' of her horse ringing out in 'the norland wind' (st 17). Because she 'shimmered like the sun' (st 20), Thomas forgets his 'real' bride. Enraged by jealousy, the nut-brown bride asks Annet what rosewater makes her so white before killing her with 'a long bodkin', or dagger. The ballad ends extraordinarily with three deaths: Thomas kills the nut-brown bride in fury, then himself in grief. Although rendered in highly stylised and dramatic ways, the ballad shows how beauty divides and destroys as well as inspires love. The nut-brown bride (note she has no name) is almost a sympathetic figure, eternally the ugly duckling to Annet's swan, but the ballad is probably best understood as a fable about choices made for the wrong reasons and the power of jealousy, based on the eternal pathos of the beautiful who die young.

Famously, sibling rivalry fosters destructive jealousy in the ballad of 'The Twa Sisters' (Lyle 29). A knight courts the elder of two sisters though, Cinderella-like, he really loves the younger. 'Vexed sair' (st 4) with envy, the jealous older sister pushes her younger rival into a river. The drowning girl pleads with her, promising her money, property, and that she 'never be nae man's wife' (st 13). She refuses: '"Your cherry cheeks an yallow hair / Gars me gae maiden for evirmair"' (st 15). The river carries the dying girl onwards: a miller's son thinks she's 'a mermaid or a swan' (st 18). When fished out of the water, her beauty is still radiant. A harper sees her beautiful corpse and strings his instrument with 'three locks o' her yallow hair' (st 25). Through his tunes, her voice miraculously lives on, bidding farewell to her parents and cursing her sister. This violent yet lyrical ballad, tersely narrated, is also a fable about beauty and innocence; but the apparent fairy tale-like rivalry between the sisters betrays dark psychological and sexual tensions.

The portrayal of women in the ballads is therefore shaped by traditional conventions and persistent archetypes. One could easily suggest that marriage and death remain the twin fates for most ballad women. Yet many songs depict women purposefully loving whom they want or, if not, expressing anxiety about their marriage destiny or loss of virginity. The power of traditional songs and stories to capture and reflect social and psychological tensions surrounding love and marriage is well documented within other cultures and their folktales. So too in the Scottish ballads 'lived' experience is often imaginatively translated into the depiction of oppressive families (especially fathers and brothers) who deliberately obstruct a young woman's path to fulfilment and happiness (see especially 'The Cruel Brother', Lyle 65). In some ballads, women are even used as political pawns between countries at war: in 'Johnie Scott' (Lyle 54), a Scotsman successfully fights for the English king's daughter ('the honour it's to Scotland come / Sore against England's will', st 23); and Lady Maisry, in the ballad of the same name, is shockingly burnt for carrying an Englishman's child (Lyle 63).

In addition to the imaginative pleasures of their stories, such female-centred ballads must have allowed the women who sang and listened to them a means of communicating fears, anxieties and hopes: both fulfilled and unhappy female characters may have acted as the symbolic projection, or sublimation, of their own feelings. Folklorists and anthropologists argue that 'women of many cultures have encoded messages crucial to them under the cover of female traditions that receive little male scrutiny'[24]. Ballads similarly reflect the capacity of traditional women's song and storytelling to portray, skilfully and subtly, situations and dilemmas which speak to women. We will end this discussion of the role of women in the ballads with an exploration of the tale of 'Burd Ellen' (Lyle 20), the most resourceful of ballad heroines, which both echoes, and takes a few steps further, the portrayal of women and female desires.

(iii) 'Burd Ellen', or why true love can never be disguised

Stanzas 1–2 As in the opening of 'Tam Lin', young women are warned about sexual transgression by an unknown narrative voice. Immediately, we see Ellen disregarding this admonition by leaving her 'father's house' to follow her lover, Lord John.

Stanzas 3–10 Ellen is determined to follow him as he rides but when he leaves without her, she disguises herself 'in page array': she will 'cross-dress' as a young boy in order to find him ('cross-dressing' is a frequent resource for medieval romance heroines; Shakespeare too gives his heroines freedom and escape through the disguise motif). The narrative develops quickly: trying to cross a river, Ellen feels 'the bairn' within her move; now we know that she is pregnant and assume Lord John to be the father. When Ellen talks to her child, we learn that the 'father ... / Cares little for us twae' (st 10).

Stanzas 11–17 Lord John stops to lift Ellen on his horse but enigmatically announces that in his castle 'is a lady ... / Will sunder you an me'. Repetition emphasises this point, and we wonder if this divisive woman is his wife. But in verses 15–18, comprised of dialogue exchanges between Ellen and John, she optimistically contradicts his fears: his worry that 'Then will ye sigh an say alas! / That ever I was a man!' is countered by her desire that 'An I hope to live an bless the day / That ever ye was a man'. Ellen blesses while John curses the hour their 'love was born'.

Stanzas 18–26 Ellen is displaced from the main narrative frame but we are reminded of her importance: her beauty, even as a page boy, exceeds that of the (formulaic) 'four and twenty gay ladies'

The Scottish Ballads

who welcome Sir John. Ellen appears vulnerable, standing alone 'at the manger'. Sitting at the side table with the other serving men, Ellen cannot eat, her 'heart's sae full of pine'. No-one knows who she is except Lord John's mother, who suspects that 'he's liker a woman big wi bairn / Than a young lord's serving man'. Ironically, John replies that he is a squire's son who 'for love' has followed him; we, the audience, know the truth of his words.

Stanzas 27–36 Ellen prepares to give birth in the stable which calls to mind the Virgin Birth. There is something natural and beautiful about how Ellen sits 'amo the great horse feet', a phrase suggesting Ellen's fragility but also the protective shelter of the stable creatures. It is Lord John's mother who hears her cries and alerts her son; an intuitive connection exists between her and Ellen. It is the mother who is Ellen's rescuer or deliverer, even though John bursts into the stable to hold his child and Ellen. Literally and symbolically, Ellen is newly clothed, 'baptised' as a new 'fair lady ... in the silk'. Her marriage and the child's christening will be the same day. Ellen acquires new identities through Lord John – social, sexual, maternal – but they are only achieved through her resilience and courage. The ballad also celebrates the power of female bonds; Lord John's mother instinctively ensures that her son will be with this woman whose true self – and true desires – she sensed.

Conclusion

This brief survey of Scottish ballad traditions began on a note of caution, describing the reticence or even reluctance with which literary critics have approached these songs. From acknowledging the way in which these texts live first and foremost through the power of song and music, we have gradually suggested the other ways in which they have meaning: from analysis of their formal 'architecture' – the interaction between stanza, rhythm and narrative structure – to exploration of their power as complex symbolic stories. Despite their contentious 'liminality' (their status as both musical and literary forms), the ballads have played an important role within Scottish literary history. Artistic figures no less than Scott and Hogg (see Appendix) have played a crucial role in shaping both the forms of the ballads which we read today and the way in which we perceive them. Perhaps because Scottish literature has frequently been placed in the intellectual and cultural shadows of other national literatures, which do not need to justify or legitimate their identity in the same way, the unique and powerful qualities of the ballad tradition have remained important to Scottish writers and critics. William Soutar (1898–1943) claimed that in the ballads 'we hear the voice of Scotland most distinctly'.[25] The Orcadian writer Edwin Muir believed that Scottish literature had lost a kind of wholeness, a unity of emotional, intellectual and spiritual senses, because of Scotland's political and cultural history. Accordingly, he loved the ballads and what '... they have given to the poetry of the world ... This world in which there is no reflection, no regard for the utility of action, nothing but pure passion seen through pure vision ... To raise immediate passion to poetry in this way, without the alleviation of reflection, without the necromancy of memory, requires a vision of unconditional clearness, like that of a child; and it may be said of the Scottish ballad-writers that they attained poetry by pure, unalleviated insight, by unquestioning artistic heroism ...'[26] Both Muir and especially his wife, Willa, wrote eloquently about the ballads; but we should be wary too of unquestioningly accepting these and other views since they reflect historically rooted philosophies and interpretations of Scottish culture. Understandably, there is a tendency to romanticise the ballads and to assume that they represent an impossibly 'pure' or 'authentic' Scottishness. Instead, we can acknowledge the role which ballads, the most traditional, and yet ambiguous, of 'art forms', played in the particular cultural drama of asserting

Scotland's status as a national literature and art. We can be grateful that ballads survive, thanks to Sir Walter Scott, a host of other distinguished collectors and scholars, and contemporary performers, storytellers and folksong revivalists.

As readers and interpreters of Scottish literature we are not the original or intended audience of the ballads. The fact that they have fallen into our hands now, between the pages of a book, should not cloud the fact that they were primarily created for enjoyment and entertainment within communities historically stretching back to the medieval period, and geographically extending from Orkney and Shetland in the north to the Borders in the south. They have travelled beyond Scotland too, carried by Scottish emigrants to be preserved, and also reworked, within cultures and communities in America, Canada and elsewhere; American country music, for example, has roots in the folk music and storytelling traditions of the Scottish, and Irish, émigré ballad culture. In that sense, ballads are always 'nearer' to us than we think. More than that, they are a living tradition. There is something both moving and enriching about our ability to interpret, analyse and, to use Jeannie Robertson's words again, so 'make live' ballads which once upon a time flourished in 'the house of the storyteller'.[27]

Appendix

(i) Sir Walter Scott, Ballad Collections and Collectors

Sir Walter Scott is probably best known as a historical novelist but his power as a writer of historical, 'romantic' fiction was partly nurtured by his love of traditional ballads. Rather like Robert Louis Stevenson, whom childhood illness compelled to create an inner, imaginative world, Scott suffered polio as a young child and spent periods of recuperation at his grandfather's farm in the Borders. Whilst there he immersed himself in local and historical legends, and discovered a work by (Bishop) Thomas Percy called *Reliques of Ancient English Poetry* (1765), containing some of 'the old minstrel ballads in the northern dialect'. Traditional ballads, such as 'Sir Patrick Spens', 'The Gaberlunzie Man', 'The Bonny Earl of Murray' and 'Sweet William's Ghost', had been printed by Percy from a seventeenth-century manuscript. This work deeply influenced Scott, embodying the appeal of medieval and traditional culture for the literary and cultural movement now known as Romanticism, and of which Scott was such an important part. As a young man, passionately interested in European literature, Scott also translated ballad poetry by a German writer called Gottfried Burger, which was itself influenced by Percy's collection. When Scott prepared his own ballad collection, *The Minstrelsy of the Scottish Border*, published in three volumes between 1802 and 1803, his fascination for ballads had long been cemented. With the help of collaborators (John Leyden, Richard Heber, William Laidlaw and James Hogg), Scott compiled his collection by transcribing the words of songs and ballads from local singers in the Borders. Indeed, Hogg's mother 'gave' Scott some traditional ballads and songs. However, it was this very process of transforming the 'sung stories' of the traditional eighteenth century Border household and farm into a printed work, a literary volume which was to enjoy tremendous popularity, that gave Scott himself pause for thought. He had given the Scottish ballads a new status as literary art and a far wider audience, or 'readership', than they had ever enjoyed, but he was anxiously aware that he had 'altered' these ballads, irrevocably in some way:

> I think I did wrong, myself in endeavouring to make the best possible set of an ancient ballad out of several copies obtained from different quarters, and that in many respects if I improved the poetry I spoiled the simplicity of the old song.[28]

The Scottish Ballads

Perhaps the most well-known expression of disquiet at what Scott had done comes from Hogg's own mother. When asked by Scott if the ballad of 'Old Maitlan' ' which she had just sung was in print, she cried: 'Oo, na, na, sir, it was never printed i' [in] the world. For my brothers an' me learned it frae auld Andrew Moor, an' he learned it frae auld Baby Mettlin, that was the housekeeper to the first laird o' Tushilaw ... It is an auld story! But mair nor that, except George Warton and James Steward, there was never ane o' my songs prentit till ye prentit them yoursel ... ant ye hae spoilt them a'thegither. They war made for singing, an' no for reading; and they're nouther right spelled nor right setten down.'[29] One can well imagine how Scott must have felt at this rebuke; but Hogg's mother felt strongly that the 'auld sangs' (note the way she implies that exact date and provenance are of no concern; instead ballads are associated with particular people) belonged to family and community. How Scott 'printed' her songs bears no relation to the way she sang and 'felt' them. In fact, she was afraid that Scott's ballad collecting 'was offending the fairies and elves, who, to her mind, were the ballad muses'.[30]

However, Scott's collection was only part of a growing tradition of song-collecting. The Union of the Parliaments between Scotland and England in 1707 influenced, both directly and indirectly, Scotland's culture; interest in, and concern for the survival of, the country's native traditions of music, song and poetry was reawakened in writers and intellectuals. The appeal of published ballad collections in this period also mirrors the huge popularity of Scots song collections printed in the earlier part of the century by the poet Allan Ramsay: *Scots Songs* (1718) and *The Tea Table Miscellany* (1724–37), as well as *The Ever Green* (1724). Although these bear the imprint of Ramsay's 'editorialising' to make the songs appropriate for polite Edinburgh society, his collection contains traditional ballads such as 'The Bonny Earl of Murray' and 'Bonny Barbara Allan'. Decades later, Robert Burns, too, took part in the song-collecting movement, contributing songs to Johnson's *Scottish Musical Museum* and Thomson's *Select Scottish Airs*. As well as the invaluable work of Francis James Child at Harvard University, in the nineteenth century there were many other important song and ballad collectors: Peter Buchan, James Maidment, George Ritchie Kinloch, Charles Kirkpatrick Sharpe, and perhaps most well known, the Glasgow writer and collector William Motherwell.

In the twentieth century, the practice of ballad and song collecting was continued in monumental ways; vast collections of transcribed Gaelic folksong and story from the Highlands and Islands were also made. In Aberdeenshire in the early part of the century the school teacher Gavin Greig and the minister James Duncan set out to preserve what they believed were the remnants of traditional song culture; but so great were the number of songs which they heard and collected (more than 3,000!) that they died before they managed to publish their material. However, what is now known as the Greig–Duncan Folksong Collection has finally been published in seven volumes, the result of painstaking research and editing by Emily Lyle and colleagues at the School of Scottish Studies in Edinburgh since Greig and Duncan's manuscripts were first rediscovered in the 1950s.

(ii) The 'Literary Ballad' in Scotland

The traditional song ballad can be contrasted with the so-called 'literary ballad', defined as an imitation of the original oral ballad form by poets who come largely from a non-oral tradition. The popularity of the 'literary ballad' was properly established in the Romantic and Victorian periods. Well-known examples of this genre are found in the poetry of William Wordsworth (e.g. *The Lyrical Ballads*), Samuel Taylor Coleridge (e.g. 'The Ancient Mariner'), John Keats (e.g. 'La Belle Dame sans Merci') and Lord Alfred Tennyson (e.g. 'Lady Clare'). This new poetic type, which explicitly imitated or implicitly alluded to the traditional ballad, introduced the ballad form to a new audience (or rather readership) drawn from 'polite' society. Accordingly, it was newly transformed or reinvented as a literary art form.

One of the earliest 'imitators' was Walter Scott, a pioneer of ballad collecting who composed some of his own. He liked to insert snatches or fragments of supposedly traditional ballads throughout his novels. In *The Antiquary*, for example, the character of old Elspeth sings a ballad about the Battle of Harlaw; and famously in *The Heart of Midlothian*, the poignant, semi-folkloric character of Madge Wildfire, a 'tall, strapping wench of eighteen or twenty, dressed fantastically ... with ... a bunch of broken feathers, a riding-skirt [or petticoat] of scarlet camlet, embroidered with tarnished flowers', is a ballad-singer. Before she dies she sings 'Proud Maisie', a ballad about a young woman told by a 'Sweet Robin' bird that only when she dies will she be a bride entering church:

> The glow-worm o'er grave and stone
> Shall light thee steady.

The owl from the steeple sing,
'Welcome, proud lady.'

Scott was skilled in making his 'new' ballads seem evocative and authentic. This is a gift shared by a famous Scottish literary imitator of the same period, James Macpherson (1736–96), who convinced an entire European reading public (including Napoleon!) that he had discovered 'ancient' Gaelic poetry about the Celtic warrior-hero, Ossian. Published in 1760, Macpherson's wonderful 'hoax' speaks to the same sensibility and interests which encouraged the literary ballad movement. In another instance of confusion over originality and imitation, the author of traditional oral ballads such as 'Sir Patrick Spens' and 'Edward, Edward' was at one time thought to be an aristocratic woman, Lady Elizabeth Wardlaw (1677–1727). The ballad of 'Hardyknute', the tale of a heroic medieval warrior defending Scotland against Norway, was attributed to her in Percy's *Reliques* and Ramsay's *The Ever Green* but it was first published anonymously as an 'authentic' and ancient ballad fragment; she 'pretended she had found this poem, written on shreds of paper, employed for what is called the bottoms of clues'. It is an intriguing fact of literary history that the ballads should have inspired this kind of *faux* creativity.

By the end of the eighteenth century, then, the boundaries between traditional and literary ballads were clearly fluid. The writer who best illustrates a combination of traditional inheritance and contemporary ballad writing is James Hogg. Hogg tells us that his mother, Margaret Laidlaw, had been 'a grand singer' of 'old songs and ballads' *(Familiar Anecdotes of Sir Walter Scott,* 1834) so the ballad compositions of *The Mountain Bard* (1807), for example, must have been shaped by the maternal ballad singing of his childhood. His later poetic collection, *The Queen's Wake* (1813), however, best fulfils his boast to be 'the king o' the mountain an' fairy school'.

In the Victorian period, the term 'ballad' still enjoyed poetic currency. Robert Louis Stevenson published a collection entitled *Ballads*, as did the poet John Davidson (1857–1909), who laced his ballad form with political irony and satire. Perhaps in the early twentieth century renaissance we best see a re-creation of the traditional ballad form and sensibility in the Scots lyric poetry of the North-East poets, Violet Jacob (1863–1946), Marion Angus (1866–1946) and Helen Cruickshank (1886–1975). Angus, for example, distils ideas of love, loss, innocence and the female voice through lyric forms which owe a strong debt to ballad dramatisation. Comparison of their poems, along with the lyrics of other modern Scottish poets such as William Soutar (1898–1943) and George Mackay Brown (1921–96), with original folk ballads can reveal the creative principles behind each, as well as inviting us to contemplate just why writers (above all in poetry but in prose too; the stories of Mackay Brown, for instance, are 'balladic' in form and spirit) have found such affinity with, and inspiration in, ballads.

(iii) Broadside Ballads

Historical accounts of traditional ballads often use the term 'broadside ballad'. This refers to a poem which was usually printed on a single sheet (a broadsheet) and widely distributed within developing towns and cities (in Scotland the first press was set up in Edinburgh by Chepman and Myllar in 1507). The subject of the broadside ballad was often some contemporary political or topical event (they could be considered the earliest form of journalism) but grew to encompass all manner of topics from sailors' homecomings to affairs of royalty. First composed in the stanza form associated with the French *balade*, these texts were subsequently called 'ballads'. Their appearance and rapid popularity was due to developments in printing technology; broadsheets became relatively cheap and efficient to produce, ensuring that the type of poetry they contained was of popular appeal. In fact, the broadside ballad eventually became a type of popular song, and music was often printed alongside the song-text. Broadside ballads first appeared in the early sixteenth century and continued to be published well into the nineteenth (and in Scotland and Ireland into the twentieth). In the earlier period, they were sold at fairs and marketplaces (and often sung at these shared, communal events). Albert Friedman helpfully sums up the later broadside ballad tradition as 'traditional balladry reformed so as better to suit the press, the city, and modern conditions'.[31]

(iv) Bothy Ballads

The North-East of Scotland is a distinctively rich area of traditional song. In the late nineteenth and early twentieth centuries, it produced a new type of folksong which is known as the 'bothy ballad'. This ballad tradition has a very specific origin and locale: the 'bothy', the living quarters (usually a stone outhouse) of unmarried farm workers in the Buchan area of Aberdeenshire. In what served as home, the farmhands composed and reinvented songs which dealt not only with the eternal ballad themes of love and courtship but with the gritty, hard realities of poorly paid farm labour, and the rituals of the agricultural season such as the *hairst* or harvest. The bothy ballad world is rooted in a specific social and rural environment, the product of newly transformed agricultural practices, and in a culture distinctive to these workers. The bothy ballads are sometimes called 'cornkisters': the corn kist was the chest, holding the corn, on which the farmworkers would 'dunt ... the heels of their tacketty boots ... in time to the tune'.[32] Their songs range from humorous to satiric accounts of farmers and the labour they demanded (wealthy farmers often treated these largely itinerant farmworkers very badly) to celebrations at harvest time and the local fairs, and tales of bothy courtships. David Buchan observes that 'the psychological function of the ballad for the folk had changed: 'the new [bothy] ballad dealt with that everyday life. Instead of ... singing about another life, the ballad singer relieved his feelings by commenting directly and sardonically on the life he led, day in, day out'.[33] One of the best contemporary singers of bothy ballads is Jock Duncan (b. 1925), a farmer's son from the Buchan area, who grew up with this song tradition. His singing has been recorded on CD, as has John Strachan's (1875–1958), another famous bothy singer. The Scottish Tradition Series has also released a recording of well-known bothy ballads by various singers.

Bibliography

General
Bold, Alan, *The Ballad* (London: Methuen, 1979)
Buchan, David (ed.), *A Scottish Ballad Book* (London and Boston: Routledge and Kegan Paul, 1973)
Buchan, David J., *The Ballad and the Folk* (London: Routledge and Kegan Paul, 1972)
Craig, David, *Scottish Literature and the Scottish People 1680–1830* (London: Chatto and Windus, 1961)
Crawford, Thomas, *Love, Labour and Liberty: The Eighteenth Century Scottish Lyric* (Cheadle: Carcanet Press, 1976)
Fergusson, Sir James, 'The Ballads' in *Scottish Poetry: A Critical Survey*, ed. James Kinsley (Cassell, 1955), pp. 99–118
Harris, Joseph (ed.), *The Ballad and Oral Literature* (Cambridge, MA and London: Harvard University Press, 1991)
Henderson, Hamish, *Alias MacAlias: Writings on Songs, Folk and Literature* (Edinburgh: Polygon, 1982)
___, 'The Oral Tradition' in *Scotland: A Concise Cultural History*, ed. Paul H. Scott (Edinburgh: Mainstream, 1993), pp. 159–71
Hodgart, Matthew John Caldwell, *The Ballads* (London: Hutchinson, 1950)
MacCarthy, William, *The Ballad Matrix: Personality, Milieu and the Oral Tradition* (Bloomington: University of Indiana Press, 1990)
McDiarmid, M.P., 'The Scottish Ballads: Appreciation and Explication' in *Proceedings of the Third International Conference on Scottish Language and Literature*, eds. R.J. Lyall and Felicity Riddy (Glasgow: University of Glasgow Press, 1981), pp. 107–24
Muir, Willa, *Living with Ballads* (London: Hogarth, 1965)
Porter, James (ed.), *The Ballad Image* (Los Angeles: University of California, 1983)

Ballad Form, Structure and Language
Anderson, Flemming G., *Commonplace and Creativity* (Odense: University Press, 1985)
Harker, James, *Fakesong: The Manufacture of British Folksong 1700 to the Present Day* (Milton Keynes: Open University Press, 1985)
Henderson, Hamish, 'At the Foot o' Yon Excellin' Brae: The Language of Scottish Folksong' in *Scotland and the Lowland Tongue*, ed. J. Derrick McClure (Aberdeen University Press, 1983), pp. 100–28

Ong, Walter, *Orality and Literacy: The Technologizing of the Word* (London: Routledge, New Accents Series, 1982)
___, *Rhetoric, Romance and Technology* (London: Cornell University Press, 1971)
Pound, Louise, *Poetic Origins and the Ballad* (New York: Russell, 1962)
Shepard, Leslie, *The Broadside Ballad: A Study in Origins and Meaning* (London: Jenkins, 1962)
Thompson, Stith (ed.), *Motif-index of folk-literature: a classification of narrative elements in folktales, ballads, myths, fables, mediaeval romances, exempla, fabliaux, jest-books, and local legends* (Bloomington: Indiana University Press, 1955–8)
Toelken, Barre, *Morning Dew and Roses: Nuance, Metaphor and Meaning in Folksongs* (Urbana: University of Illinois Press, 1995)
Wurzbach, Natascha and Salz, Simone M., *Motif Index of the Child Corpus: The English and Scottish Popular Ballad* (Berlin: Walter and Gruyter, 1995)

Ballad Music
Bronson, Bertrand Harris, *The Ballad as Song* (Berkeley, CA: University of California Press, 1969)
___, *Traditional Tunes of the Child Ballads* (Princeton, NJ: University Press, 1959–72)
___, *The Singing Tradition of Child's Popular Ballads* (Princeton NJ: University Press, 1976)
Campbell, Katherine and McVicar, Ewan, *Traditional Scottish Songs and Music*, with accompanying CD (St Andrews: Leckie and Leckie, 2001)
Collinson, Francis, *The Traditional and National Music of Scotland* (London: Routledge, 1966)
Crawford, Thomas, 'Lowland Song and Popular Tradition in the Eighteenth Century' in *The History of Scottish Literature Volume 2: 1660–1800*, ed. Andrew Hook (Aberdeen: University Press, 1987), pp. 123–41
Douglas, Sheila (ed.), *The Sang's the Thing: Voices from Lowland Scotland* (Edinburgh: Polygon, 1992)
Munro, Ailie, *The Democratic Muse: Folk Music Revival in Scotland* (Aberdeen: Scottish Cultural Press, 1996)
___, *Jeannie Robertson: Emergent Singer, Transformative Voice* (East Linton: Tuckwell Press, 1999)
Purser, John, *Scotland's Music* (Edinburgh: Mainstream, 1992)

Women in the Ballads
Brown, Mary Ellen, 'Old Singing Women and the Canons of Scottish Balladry and Song' in *A History of Scottish Women's Writing*, ed. Douglas Gifford and Dorothy MacMillan (Edinburgh: University Press, 1997), pp. 44–57
Dugaw, Dianne, *Warrior Women and Popular Balladry 1650–1850* (Cambridge: University Press, 1989)
Freedman, Jean R., 'With Child: Illegitimate Pregnancy in Scottish Traditional Ballads' in *Folklore* 24, no. 1 (1991), pp. 3–18
Petrie, Elaine, 'What a Voice! Women, Repertoire and Loss in the Singing Tradition' in *A History of Scottish Women's Writing*, ed. Douglas Gifford and Dorothy MacMillan (Edinburgh: University Press, 1997), pp. 262–73
Symonds, Deborah A., *Weep Not for Me: Women, Ballads & Infanticide in Early Modern Scotland* (University Park, Pennsylvania: Pennsylvania State University Press, 1997)

The Ballads and the Supernatural
Briggs, Katherine, *The Fairies in Tradition and Literature* (London: Routledge and Kegan Paul, 1967)
Henderson, Lizanne, 'The Road to Elfland: Fairy Belief and the Child Ballads' in *The Ballad in Scottish History*, ed. Edward J. Cowan (East Linton: Tuckwell Press, 2000), pp. 54–72
____, Henderson, Lizanne, and Edward J. Cowan (eds), *Scottish Fairy Belief: a history* (East Linton: Tuckwell Press, 2001)
Wimberly, L.C., *Folklore in English and Scottish Ballads* (New York: Dover, 1928; rpt. 1965)

The Ballad in History
Cowan, Edward J. (ed.), *The Ballad in Scottish History* (East Linton: Tuckwell Press, 2000)
____, (ed.), *The People's Past* (Edinburgh: Polygon, 1980)
Crawford, Thomas, *Society and the Lyric: A Study of the Song Culture of Eighteenth Century Scotland* (Edinburgh: Scottish Academic Press, 1979)
MacCarthy, William B., 'The Polarization of Scots Society and Ballad Collecting in the Early Nineteenth Century' in *Lore & Language*, vol. 12 (1994), pp. 129–146
Mackenzie, M.L., 'The Great Ballad Collectors: Percy, Herd and Ritson' in *Studies in Scottish Literature*, Volume II, no.4.
Niles, John D., and Long, Eleanor R., 'Context and Loss in Scottish Ballad Tradition' in *Folklore* 45, no. 2 (1986), pp. 93–109
Rieuwerts, Sigrid, 'Allan Ramsay and the Scottish Ballads' in

Aberdeen University Review, Vol. LVIII, 1, no. 201 (Spring, 1999), pp. 29–41

Vansina, Jan, *Oral Tradition as History* (Madison: University of Wisconsin Press, 1985)

Ballad Recordings – Discography

Scottish Ballads. An Interactive CD-ROM featuring sound, images, lyrics and commentary. Directed by Ted Cowan (Glasgow: University of Glasgow, 2004)

Folksongs of North East Scotland: Songs from the Greig–Duncan Collection (Edinburgh: Greentrax Recordings, 1995), Compact Disc

It Fell on a Day: Volume 17, The Voice of the People (London: Topic Records, 1998), Compact Disc

Mary Macqueen's Ballads (Edinburgh: Scottish Text Society, undated), Audio Cassette

O'er his Grave the Grass Grew Green: Volume 3, The Voice of the People (London: Topic Records, 1998), Compact Disc

Scottish Tradition 5: The Muckle Sangs (Edinburgh: Greentrax Recordings, 1992), Compact Disc

The Shepherd's Song: Border Ballads (Cockenzie, East Lothian: Greentrax Recordings, c.1998), Compact Disc

Ten Scottish Ballads (Glasgow: Scotsoun, c.1985), Audio Cassette

Ballads on the Internet

Scottish Ballads weblog:
www.springthyme.co.uk/weblog/scotsballadblog.shtml

Scotland's Child Ballads Site:
www.springthyme.co.uk/ballads/childballads_enter.html

The Scottish Ballads:
www.fsu.edu/~speccoll/ballad.htm

Bibliography of the Ballads:
www.bartleby.com/212/1700.html

Glasgow Broadside Ballads – The Murray Collection:
www.broadsideballads.gallowayfolk.co.uk/index.htm

Oral Tradition:
www.oraltradition.org/bibliography/index.asp?alpha=C

Scottish Storytelling Centre:
www.scottishstorytellingcentre.co.uk/

Traditional Music and Song Association of Scotland
www.tmsa.org.uk/

Folk Resources on the World Wide Web:
pers-www.wlv.ac.uk/~in2021/folkres.htm

Celtic and Scottish Studies, Edinburgh University:
www.celtscot.ed.ac.uk/

NOTES

1. David Buchan, *The Ballad and the Folk* (London: Routledge & Kegan Paul, 1972), p. 1.
2. Willa Muir, *Living With Ballads* (London: Hogarth Press, 1965), p. 18.
3. Thomas Pettitt, 'Introduction: The Ballad as Narrative', in *The Ballad as Narrative: studies in the ballad traditions of England, Scotland, Germany, and Denmark*, edited by Flemming G. Andersen, Otto Holzapfel, and Thomas Pettitt (Odense: Odense University Press, 1982), p. 3.
4. William James Entwhistle, *European Balladry* (Oxford: Oxford University Press, 1939), p. 13.
5. Bertrand Harris Bronson, *The Ballad as Song* (Berkeley: University of California Press, 1969), p. 37.
6. James Porter and Herschel Gower, *Jeannie Robertson. Emergent Singer, Transformative Voice* (East Linton: Tuckwell Press, 1995), p. 53.
7. Lines taken from William Dunbar, 'The Tretis of the Tua Mariit Wemen and the Wedo'; Gerard Manley Hopkins, 'Inversnaid'.
8. Vladimir Propp, *Morphology of the Folktale* (Austin: University of Texas Press, 1968), p. 21.
9. Propp, p. 20.
10. Entwhistle p. 27.
11. Muir, p. 33.
12. Muir, p. 129.
13. James Reed, 'The Border Ballads', in *The People's Past. Scottish Folk, Scottish History*, ed. Edward J. Cowan (Edinburgh: Edinburgh University Student Publications Boad, 1980), p. 18.
14. Ian A. Olson, 'Just How Was the Bonny Earl of Moray Killed?' in *The Ballad in Scottish History*, ed. Edward J. Cowan (East Linton: Tuckwell Press, 2000), p. 36.
15. Cited in Olson, p. 36.

16 See p. 281 of the Notes to Emily Lyle's Canongate edition.
17 M.J.C. Hodgart, *The Ballads* (London: Hutchinson, 1950), p. 116.
18 Maria Tatar, *The Hard Facts of the Grimms Fairy Tales* (Princeton, NJ: Princeton University Press, 1987), pp. 55–6.
19 Muir, p. 130
20 The Scottish writer Eric Linklater (1899–1974) has a beautiful short story version of the selkie legend called 'Sealskin Trousers'. See also David Thomson, *The People of the Sea. Celtic Tales of the Sea-Folk* (Edinburgh: Canongate Classics, 2001).
21 Mary Ellen Brown, 'Old Singing Women and the Canons of Scottish Balladry and Song', in *A History of Scottish Women's Writing*, eds Douglas Gifford and Dorothy McMillan (Edinburgh: Edinburgh University Press, 1997), p. 51.
22 Brown, p. 47.
23 Lyle ed., p. 271
24 *Feminist Messages. Coding in Women's Folk Culture*, ed. Joan Newlon Radner (Urbana: University of Illinois Press, 1993), p. vii.
25 Quoted in Roderick Watson, *The Literature of Scotland* (Basingstoke: Macmillan, 1984), p. 418.
26 Edwin Muir, *Selected Prose*, chosen, introduced, and with a memoir by George Mackay Brown (London: John Murray, 1987), pp. 14, 15.
27 Second quotation is from the *Carmina Gadelica*, cited in Adam Nicholson, *Sea Room* (London: HarperCollins, 2002), p. 258.
28 Letter to Motherwell, 3 May 1825, cited in Alan Bold, *The Ballad*, p. 1.
29 Hogg, *Familiar Anecdotes of Sir Walter Scott* (1834).
30 Albert B. Friedman, *The Ballad Revival. Studies in the Influence of Popular on Sophisticated Poetry* (Chicago: University of Chicago Press, 1961), p. 8.
31 Friedman, p. 45.
32 Buchan, p. 262.
33 Buchan, p. 268.